HEADTRASH 2

**Dealing with
and Overcoming
Other People's Junk**

*Tish Squillaro
and Timothy I. Thomas*
with Alan Sharavsky

GREENLEAF
BOOK GROUP PRESS

Published by Greenleaf Book Group Press
Austin, Texas
www.gbgpress.com

Distributed by Greenleaf Book Group

For ordering information or special discounts for bulk purchases, please contact
Greenleaf Book Group at PO Box 91869, Austin, TX 78709, 512.891.6100.

Design and composition by Greenleaf Book Group
Cover design by Jason Haker
Cartoons Concept by Alan Sharavsky and Illustrations by Jaki Katz Ashford

Cataloging-in-Publication data is available.

Print ISBN: 978-1-62634-274-3

eBook ISBN: 978-1-62634-275-0

Part of the Tree Neutral® program, which offsets the number of trees
consumed in the production and printing of this book by taking
proactive steps, such as planting trees in direct proportion to the
number of trees used: www.treeneutral.com

TreeNeutral®

Printed in the United States of America on acid-free paper

15 16 17 18 19 20   10 9 8 7 6 5 4 3 2 1

First Edition

DEDICATION

To my family, friends, and colleagues who have allowed me to probe and capture the inner workings around HeadTrash and who have shared how it has impacted their lives and the lives of those around them. It has been a wonderful experience building *HeadTrash 2* because of its amazing focus on working with others, and because it has deepened my relationships with each of you. Thank you for letting me learn through you.

To my beautiful children, Berlyn and Jack, for teaching me new things about life and love all the time, and my soul mate and love, Matt, who so graciously deals with all my junk!

—Tish

To my coaching clients over the years who have courageously faced their HeadTrash and done the difficult work to transform their lives and careers.

It has been an honor and privilege to be inspired by you.

—Tim

CONTENTS

How to take out someone else's garbage . . . What is
HeadTrash, Part 2? Seeing it outside of ourselves . . .
Defining the problem . . . Crossing the Line: "Not to
be confused with" . . . A preview: what you can expect
from this book . . . A caveat: to help, not to label . . .
HeadTrash911.com

Case History: When silence is deadly . . . Expressions of
anger: Eight signs to look for at home and at work . . .
A word of caution about anger: Calm down, and consider
outside help . . . *Behind the Scenes with Tish & Tim:*
Anger Anecdote—Her politics versus their marriage . . . An
Anger Checklist and Comparison: How to identify anger
HeadTrash in someone you know . . . HeadTrash Alert!
A Quick Quiz on Anger . . . The counterintuitive side of
anger: Use it constructively . . . Advising the person with
the HeadTrash of anger . . . Change your mind, literally:
Think your way out of anger . . . Preparation reduces
agitation and instigation . . . Are you perfect? Is anyone?
Reality, anger reducer 1 . . . Laughter, anger reducer 2 . . .
Avoid it today. Confront it tomorrow in a calmer state

ACKNOWLEDGMENTS

We wish to acknowledge a talented group of professionals who were integral in helping us develop this book.

As with our first book, we were delighted to work with Alan Sharavsky, who continues to amaze us with his ability to bring humor and creative insight to the concept of HeadTrash.

We are grateful to our colleague Penny Zenker who contributed her invaluable expertise as a strategic business coach and productivity expert to the pages of this book.

We were blessed to work with Hilary Hinzmann, our thought-provoking editor, whose commitment to excellence strengthened our thinking and our writing.

We also wish to thank Jason Haker, our cover designer, and Jaki Katz Ashford, our illustrator, for creatively capturing the themes of HeadTrash in their work.

It is also important to acknowledge our clients and friends who have courageously faced their HeadTrash and helped others to do the same.

CONTRIBUTORS

In writing this second volume of the *HeadTrash* series, we have benefited from the contributions of co-author Alan Sharavsky (he also co-authored the first volume) and fellow consultant Penny Zenker.

Alan Sharavsky, Co-Author

Before Alan Sharavsky joined our team, *HeadTrash* was just a concept, a journey minus a map. As co-author, Alan Sharavsky turned our experiences and strategies into the engaging and practical prose that became our book, and he has done the same for this one as well. He's been a valuable contributor to the Head-Trash enterprise. Alan is the author of *Boarding School Bastard*, a memoir about his childhood at Girard College, an orphanage for fatherless boys. He's also written and produced for numerous TV networks and publications, including Viacom, Discovery Channel, the *Philadelphia Inquirer*, NPR affiliate WHYY, and *AdWeek*. In his day job, Alan is president of Sharavsky Communications, a full service advertising, PR, and digital marketing services company that has worked with brands such as Tylenol, Splenda, The Philadelphia 76ers, and Hollywood Casino.

Penny Zenker, Strategic Business Coach and Productivity Expert

Few know how to help people make the most of their time like Penny Zenker. She's the creator of the P10: Productivity

Accelerator System, a time and energy management system that teaches people about the 10 Core Drivers of Productivity: purpose, language, physiology, focus, planning, process, priority, progress, measurement, and proactivity. A productivity expert, business coach, international speaker and trainer, radio personality, and author, she embodies the word productive! We've invited Penny to comment throughout the book in sections entitled "Penny's Perspective," to give you another point of view from a premier business coach on the effects of HeadTrash and how best to overcome them.

Recognizing HeadTrash in Yourself and Others

How to take out someone else's garbage

Ideally everybody should take out their own trash, including dealing with the mental junk that all too readily accumulates in people's heads. We call this mental junk HeadTrash, ways of thinking and feeling that, left unchecked, lead to counter-productive behaviors. Life is not ideal, however, and reality often dictates that we have to deal with the garbage in someone else's head. How often have you experienced something like the following?

"Handle with care."

That was the phrase running through your mind like a car alarm every second you spent drafting the new proposal for your boss. Not that you could ever afford to be laissez faire, or simply lazy, working for such a demanding and brilliant woman. But this particular statement of work had seven figures attached to it, making it crucial that you dotted every "i," crossed every "t," and spotted anything that could be misread or seemed askew.

This was the biggest project you'd been involved with to date for the company, and you would be presenting it shoulder to shoulder with your boss. You had an extra-vested interest in getting it right, especially as you'd be strutting your stuff at the presentation to demonstrate your value.

Which is why it was so odd that the part of the presentation your boss had drafted misinterpreted a client request during the discovery phase of the assignment. After you double and triple checked your notes, and then queried someone else who was at the meeting, you were certain the section needed to be changed. That meant telling your boss of just five months that she was wrong. Not wanting to shine a brighter spotlight on the problem than necessary, you decided to wait until your scheduled meeting to review the whole document with her.

Section by section, point by point, the two of you walked through the proposal until you landed on the passage in question. You took a breath and said, "I think we may have misconstrued something here. It doesn't seem to line up with the rest of the proposal. So I drafted an alternate version of this section, just in case." You made a point to emphasize the word "we" to share the responsibility, hoping it would soften the blow.

She was having none of it: "I don't think so. I clearly recall the way they described this, and I would think I'd know the best way to present it. Let's leave it as I wrote it."

Expecting the pushback, you played the new-employee-in-search-of-wisdom card and said, "Of course, but would you take a second to review what I wrote, just for my understanding?"

She nodded impatiently, snapping the page out of your hand. But as she read your revision, her eyes widened. Unconsciously, she let out a brief "hmmm," an involuntary affirmation that she now saw her error—*the very thing that you had seen first.* You waited for her to pat you on the back, praising your diligence and brilliance. Instead she dismissed you, saying, "Well, I suppose you could interpret it that way, too. That's not how I would do it, but we'll use your version for now."

What? *WHAT!?!* "For now?" The gall of her, to act as if she was throwing you a bone! She was wrong and she knew it. But she couldn't admit that you were right. What arrogance, you thought.

But at least now you know what you're dealing with when you interact with your boss. Or do you?

Arrogance is one of seven types of what we call HeadTrash: distorted ways of thinking and feeling that engender counterproductive behaviors and interfere with your functioning in the world. They are: anger, arrogance, control, fear, guilt, insecurity, and paranoia. In trying to understand which HeadTrash was driving your boss's behavior, you might think arrogance a natural conclusion. After all, this leader exhibits many of the hallmarks of arrogance, as we described it in the checklist from our first book, *HeadTrash: Cleaning out the junk that stands between you and success.*

Is overly proud. Is certain he or she knows what to do, and does not invite help.
Feels threatened easily. His or her way is the best way. In fact, the only way!
Focuses on "I," even as he or she pretends to be interested in others.

But the HeadTrash that actually provoked this episode, and what probably drives much of how this boss reacts, is insecurity.

Offers answers without asking the probing questions.
Has a hard time allowing anyone else into the process.
Is quick to grab credit.
Can't find anyone good enough to help carry the ball.

In reality, this seemingly self-composed leader is unsure of herself, particularly in the presence of an employee whose careful, accurate work makes him seem like a threat instead of a supporting player. Understanding the difference between arrogance and insecurity—and the five other HeadTrash categories—is critical to knowing how to respond effectively to this boss's HeadTrash, and in turn the HeadTrashes of others you live and work with. And that's why we wrote this book.

Over and over—at our workshops, during TV and radio interviews, in our engagements as corporate coaches—variants of one question came up. "What do I do if my spouse, boss, colleague, employee, teenage child, (fill in the blank) has HeadTrash? How do I work with it or around it, and more important help correct it, so that this person and I can make progress together?"

That question—how to handle someone else's HeadTrash—is the reason we wrote this book. After all, no one is an island. Whether you're part of a team that's been stalled while trying to initiate a company project, or you're not seeing eye to eye with your spouse on the family budget, one person may have a stumbling block that prevents everyone from moving forward. Thus one person's HeadTrash becomes everyone else's obstacle course. In other words, as long as we must interact with other people to complete anything meaningful personally or professionally, it may not be enough to resolve our own self-defeating thought patterns and actions. To be effective, we not only have to work on ourselves, we also have to help the people we rely on to do the same.

What is *HeadTrash, Part 2*? Seeing it outside of ourselves

In our first book, we described HeadTrash as the thought patterns and emotional tendencies that hinder our ability to respond to problems productively. Think of it as your subconscious mind holding a megaphone that continually amplifies the negative scripts and beliefs that influence your decisions and form a portion of your identity. Those places where you feel stalled, where you're repeating no-win behaviors, that's your HeadTrash talking. We wrote this book because we realized that if we wanted to close the loop, and HeadTrash-proof the world, we had an obligation to help people detect and lessen HeadTrash in others as well. The good news is that the obstructions that cause us problems are the very same ones we're likely to see in others, too. The seven deadly HeadTrashes are universal, whether you're trying to identify your own or someone else's.

As we pointed out in our first book, we've seen these sinkholes wreck more careers and undermine more businesses than any others. Yes, we humans have other unwelcome, unproductive foibles. However, these seven psychological and behavioral modes have the power to undo even the most skilled and well-intentioned individuals, often working so far below the surface that the people driven by them can't see the root causes of their problems. They're the malign forces that most trouble people in their personal and professional lives.

fear ARROGANCE

Insecurity   CONTROL

Anger   *Guilt*

paranoia

In our experience with leaders in hundreds of companies, we've seen that different forms of HeadTrash often produce similar symptoms and that you have to identify the underlying cause to apply an effective treatment in a particular case. Fortunately, probing beneath the symptoms can reveal what is really causing them. But to classify the form(s) of HeadTrash troubling your boss, friend, or loved one, you'll have to look deeper than the surface warning signs.

It's thoroughly human to experience insecurity, guilt, or even paranoia on occasion. What's abnormal and counterproductive is when such thoughts and feelings become the norm in yourself or someone you have to deal with every day. So if you can help someone recognize and act on their HeadTrash, you'll be doing them a huge favor.

DEFINING THE PROBLEM

Do you know someone who lives with a chronic ailment without ever having it diagnosed or treated by a doctor? Without knowing the real cause of the problem, he or she only knows how to avoid exacerbating the discomfort. Some people "accommodate" back pain by not lifting grocery bags. Some have a sinus condition they say prevents them from living in certain parts of the U.S. Others have foot pain, restricting the amount of exercise they can do. What these and many other illnesses have in common is that their symptoms have more than one possible root cause that can be identified and treated effectively. And yet these people proceed on autopilot, using work-around behaviors instead of addressing the underlying problem. Is the back pain the result of a herniated disc, scoliosis or sciatica? Can it be treated with surgery, a steroid shot, or physical therapy?

In some ways, that's what living with HeadTrash is like. The people who have it may know their symptoms (or not), and often expect the people around them to accommodate their behaviors. You, on the other hand, want to help that person and the people around him or her by pointing out behaviors that are unproductive. But in order to recommend a remedy, you first have to "Define the Problem." Differentiating between normal misunderstandings versus a debilitating blind spot that won't change without effort is the first step to working with another person's "stuff." The trick is knowing when a behavior is "crossing the line."

CROSSING THE LINE: "NOT TO BE CONFUSED WITH"

Oh, human emotions. You can be so puzzling, so difficult to fathom. Is it abnormal to feel a little fear when you're about to present a multimillion-dollar proposal to your boss? Is it wrong to want to exert some control over a major home-improvement project that will affect your whole family and likely wreak havoc on your daily lives? Do these feelings make you or someone you care about an insecure person, or a control freak unable to delegate? Hardly. What we talk about in our HeadTrash seminars are the differences between normal emotions and behaviors on the one hand, and on the other hand dysfunctional patterns of behavior that have a harmful effect on the team, the business, or the family, and on one's credibility in that context.

In our workshops, the way we help people distinguish the difference is by using the following expression: "Not to be confused with." For instance, control-freak behavior should not be confused with developing the essential business risk systems that any good executive applies to maintain quality standards, or with the age-appropriate discipline that children need to grow up well. Before you jump in and start offering coaching, make sure you're not confusing reasonable reactions with unproductive behaviors. To help you identify the difference, here are some key distinctions:

- Fear, not to be confused with being cautious or prudent.

- Arrogance, not to be confused with self-confidence.

- Insecurity, not to be confused with humility. Humility is a virtue. Insecurity is a disease!

- Control, not be confused with necessary checks and balances in an organization or with appropriate behavior limits in a family or social setting.

- Anger, not to be confused with passion or a sense of urgency for getting things right.

- Guilt, not be confused with genuine caring and compassion for others.

- Paranoia, not be confused with a healthy skepticism about possible hidden motives and unstated agendas in human interactions.

In other words, take a second look, and read the rest of the book before attempting to fix something that may not be broken.

A preview: What you can expect from this book

Here's an overview of what's ahead, and how you and the people you want to help can get the most out of *HeadTrash 2*. Each chapter covers one of the seven HeadTrashes in depth. But first, a word of caution. The temptation will be for you to see a HeadTrash, and exult, "Yes, control! That's it! That's my spouse's HeadTrash. Let's get to work!" Not so fast, Early Bird.

What you think is control may actually be arrogance. And some behaviors may be what we call "Cocktails," where two HeadTrashes come together to make their own potent brew.

As a result, we highly recommend that you read the *whole* book, or at very least a few chapters that you think line up with your colleague's or loved one's behaviors before you jump to conclusions. To make that as easy as possible for you, we've included common elements in every chapter:

CASE HISTORY

Effective teachers, preachers, parents, sales people and leaders all know that the best way to make a point is to tell a story. We've collected many real-life episodes and categorized them to help you see how particular HeadTrashes operate. To protect people's privacy we have disguised individuals and situations in various ways, but everything we describe is something we've encountered in our lives and careers, usually multiple times.

SIGNS TO LOOK FOR AT HOME AND AT WORK

After living or working with someone for a while, you get to know and accept their idiosyncrasies. But what you've to come to accept as "just the way Bob is" may be a flashing neon sign of his HeadTrash. Other telltale behaviors may fly way under the radar. This section shines a light on the signs of the HeadTrash in question.

BEHIND THE SCENES WITH TISH & TIM

Each "behind the scenes" is a story taken from our personal experiences with family, friends, and clients. These passages outline events we've lived through or have been very close to, and share our ongoing learning from them. That process never stops for us, and it should become a regular habit for you, as well. HeadTrash is a part of human nature. We all have some, and no one can ever be entirely free of it. At the same time, we have seen again and again that individuals can dramatically improve their functioning by learning to manage, and even transcend, their inevitable human HeadTrash, and that they can help others to do the same. We will show you how to do so in this book.

CHECKLIST AND COMPARISON: HOW TO IDENTIFY HEADTRASH IN SOMEONE YOU KNOW

Think of this as the evil twin section, a chart that contrasts negative HeadTrash behaviors with positive counterpart behaviors. For example, insecurity can look like caution. But caution is productive and preventative, a preemptive measure which doesn't derail progress. Insecurity is a personal moat you can't swim out of. We compare the differences between each HeadTrash and its better angel.

A QUICK QUIZ ON EACH HEADTRASH

Every chapter includes a brief diagnostic quiz to assess whether the person you're trying to help has the HeadTrash in question. If possible, that person should do the quiz. But if that's not possible, because he or she won't cooperate, or because you're not in a position to ask them to do so, you can exercise your sympathetic imagination and take the quiz as if you were standing in their shoes. If you know the person reasonably well, you're likely to be more than accurate enough.

TISH AND TIM SPEAK UP

For each HeadTrash, we give you a quick sound bite from our personal discussions. Sometimes we agree; other times its point/ counter point.

ADVISING THE PERSON WITH HEADTRASH

This is where we put our money where your mouth is, sharing specific steps to take to help your friend, family member, or colleague begin to deal with their HeadTrash. In this coach's playbook you'll find ideas to help you initiate discussions, cognitive techniques to interrupt counterproductive behaviors, and counsel gleaned from our years as executive and personal coaches.

A caveat: To help, not to label

The purpose of this book is to improve daily life, to help you and the people you care about recognize the unproductive behaviors and thoughts that typically hold human beings back from achieving their full potential. To do that, we've categorized seven forms of HeadTrash that we see in our daily work. These undesirable traits are so common, by the way, that participants in our seminars usually name them seconds after we start to describe them. But it's not our goal to label people. Rather, we want to help everyone recognize and work with their own behaviors, using proven approaches that have been successful for our clients.

HeadTrash911.com

Our web site, www.HeadTrash911.com, serves as a complement to this book. If you or the person you're coaching want to learn more about HeadTrash, please visit the site for additional resources including our blog, videos, and an online test to diagnose which HeadTrash you're dealing with.

Anger—It's All the Rage, All the Time

"He's impossible live to with. I feel like I'm always walking on egg shells, because I never know what's going to set him off. We'll be having a conversation about something that I thought was insignificant, but if my opinion doesn't match his, he goes off. He's like a volcano that erupts without warning. And when he does, it's very bad."

You've heard the expression, "I have a button on me about that." There are particular topics or specific behaviors that rattle your cage. Maybe you hate it when people talk loudly on their cell phones in public places. Perhaps you're intolerant of braggarts who boast about their income and social standing. Or if you hear one more person raving about the movie *Frozen* and singing "Let It Go," you may go postal. We all have things that push our buttons. But because our list of annoyances is usually short, our friends and loved ones know where not to go, or how to tread there gently. We're all entitled to a few pet peeves, and to get mad from time to time.

But with the angry person, anything can be the trigger. That leaves the rest of us spending our time guessing where the trip-wire is. A seemingly friendly conversation can veer down a dark path, in one person's mind, and lead to seething rage.

"Can I get three guesses? I just don't want
to apologize for the wrong thing again."

In defining anger, the American Psychological Association quotes Charles Spielberger, PhD, a psychologist who specializes in studying it: "Anger is an emotional state that varies in intensity from mild irritation to intense fury and rage." That's a good general description. But for the person with the HeadTrash of anger, it's not a temporary state, it's a permanent condition.

"The anger is always there," says Tish. "That's one of the frustrations for everyone else who deals with the angry person, because you think you did something to create the anger. But here's the secret. The anger was there from the beginning, and it keeps festering."

And lest you think there's only one mode of expression for anger—verbal or physical confrontation—think again, says Tim. He refers to the brilliant book *Crucial Conversations*, by Kerry Patterson and Joseph Grenny, who talk about two common and disturbing expressions of anger: violence and silence.

"When we think of extreme anger, we think of violent behavior, which includes someone raising their voice or raising their hands, acting out verbally or physically. But silence and freezing out others can be equally damaging. That's when the enraged person shuts down and disengages," says Tim.

A simple illustration is when you're in a heated argument on the phone, and the other person hangs up before the conversation is done. Now you're left with no place to put your feelings and express your view. Tim says, "That's aggressive! When the stakes are high, and emotions are boiling over, people with the Head-Trash of Anger may use obvious violence or silence. The behaviors may look different, but they're two sides of the same coin."

Penny's Perspective

People with deep-seated anger tend to swing from anger to sadness or apathy. The truth is that neither is sustainable, which is why they pinball from one state to the other. I've seen people who had seething anger for years let go of the rage when they changed their lifestyle and got out of an unhealthy relationship they were tolerating. They made peace and moved on. And like a cloud lifting, the anger dissipated.

Case History: When silence is deadly

Overhearing the conversations between Brad and his fourteen-year-old son, Tommy, was like listening to an engine struggling to turn over. Sputtering, stalling, they spoke recognizable words, but they never connected, never actually engaged. Both of them were musicians, so you would think their mutual love of music would be a bond. But it became another source of tension. Dad, a hometown guitar hero, played studio sessions on a few classic rock albums in his day, when his band also toured as an opening act for legends like David Bowie, Foreigner and Def Leppard. But that day passed when Brad and his wife, Megan, started a family. Brad put his rock star dream on hold as he traded his axe for a socket wrench and became a mechanic.

When Tommy hit puberty and began to harbor his own musical ambitions, he started to snap "Boring!" every time Brad mentioned an old gig or picked up his guitar to practice. Tommy played the bass and worshiped jazz musicians. "Rock sucks, Dad. Most of these guys have no technical skills. It's all has-beens and never-weres," Tommy insisted, in obvious slaps at his father's career. But dad was about to get his second chance.

His agent called. The band, which hadn't played a gig in 15 years, was being asked to join a reunion tour with three other groups of similar vintage. The tour would take Brad away from home for six months. But it was an opportunity he felt he couldn't turn down. If things went well enough, this might become the launching pad for a few new songs, if not a whole album. It was a rare second chance. Brad and Megan agreed he should do it. It wasn't long before Brad climbed on the tour bus, guitar case in hand, and waved goodbye.

At home, Tommy began acting out. Mom got a call from the school guidance counselor, alerting her that he was skipping classes and in danger of failing chemistry. That, combined with repeated evenings when Tommy came home after his curfew (once sneaking out of his bedroom through the window), led to bitter phone battles with Brad between shows.

Those six months zoomed by, or dragged on, depending on whether you were the guitar deity resurrected or the mom wrestling with her son's skirmishes with school administrators. After Brad returned home, he was still balancing "normal life" with fanning the spark the tour had rekindled. There was talk of major producers backing studio projects for the band, maybe another tour. But there was also no way to ignore the gulf that had widened between Brad and Tommy.

The most disturbing part of it wasn't apparent right away, lost in the exciting reverberations from the tour. Tommy had stopped talking to his father. Brad wasn't sure about it at first. It was easy to miss since Tommy went out of his way to avoid him, skipping meals or vanishing into his room the second he came home.

Then one day Tommy needed a ride to a friend's house. "Do you mind taking him to Mary's house?" Megan asked Brad.

"Mom, I'd rather ride with you," Tommy said.

"I'm happy to take you, Tommy," Brad said.

"Tommy, I can't take you today," Megan said. "I have to be at work in 15 minutes and it's in the opposite direction."

"That's okay, Mom," Tommy said. "I can see Mary another time." He left the room. He didn't acknowledge his father's presence, didn't so much as turn in his direction. The hostile avoidance made it official. Tommy wasn't talking to his father.

And his mother, happy that Tommy was being polite to her for a change, didn't realize that in allowing Tommy to leave the room without being disciplined for giving his father the silent treatment, she was enabling that behavior and letting him play his parents off against each other. In truth, neither Brad nor Megan wanted to confront the problem, for fear of making it worse.

Tommy's anger at his father for leaving the family to go on tour manifested itself as a deafening silence. The root cause of Tommy's anger was driven by his feelings of abandonment which led him to shut down. He expressed his discontent with his dad by not expressing anything at all. Some say that the opposite of love is hate. But the truth is that love's true polar opposite is indifference, the kind of frosty apathy Tommy's silence was showing. Unconsciously he was acting out the phrase "you're dead to me" with a silence that would go on for weeks. Anger, you see, has many forms, and what these parents were ignoring was among the most caustic.

Eventually, Tommy resumed talking with his father again, but only in the most cursory ways, and only when absolutely necessary. As anyone who's seen passive-aggressive behavior knows, there's a difference between conversation and connection. As soon as Tommy got old enough, he moved out of his parents' house and distanced himself from his father, seeing him only at essential family events like funerals and weddings. For all intents and purposes, they were estranged. No one acknowledged the break publicly, making excuses for why Tommy didn't visit his parents on the holidays. Everyone knew what was really happening. Yet no one did anything to correct it. That's how anger can poison relationships.

ANGER: WHERE DOES IT COME FROM?
AN EXCERPT FROM OUR FIRST HEADTRASH BOOK

Anger is really a verb disguised as a noun. It's such a powerful emotion, so outwardly expressed and active, it's normal to think the angry person is little more than a human tripwire, a powder keg with a short fuse.

But the truth is far more complex, as we demonstrated in our first book.

Persistent anger, psychologists report, has personal roots. Perennially angry people are often angriest with themselves. Steady anger is anguish turned outward. And while the reasons are as individual as people themselves, there are five main sources of anger. To understand and work with an angry person, it's helpful to know where the hostility comes from. So we've included an important section from our first book, *HeadTrash! Cleaning Out the Junk That Stands between You and Success.*

The Five Real Sources of Anger—they're Not What You Think.

1. REGRET

A relentless sense of discontent with one's life is a tough burden to carry. Perhaps you know someone who lacks educational credentials, and subconsciously spends all day feeling less worthy than colleagues with MBAs from top-tier schools. Maybe he thinks he hasn't been providing for his family the way he should have. Or he's made a few business mistakes that begin gnawing at him whenever the stress level rises. Not making their own mental grade could be causing someone you have to interact with or care about to unconsciously take it out on the people around them.

2. HANGING ONTO PAST WOUNDS

This is sensitive stuff, but it needs to be said. Even some of the most powerful people have pain in their past, unresolved issues that they may unknowingly be bringing to work. A history with abusive parents, teachers, therapists, or spiritual advisors can show up as contentious feelings toward people in senior management. A divorce that ended poorly can make a person touchy in situations that are reminiscent of the prior relationship. A devastating experience at a previous job can put someone on constant alert, even when there's no present threat.

3. LACK OF SELF WORTH

Closely related to disappointment, as a source of anger, is low self-esteem. People with low self-esteem often feel as if they are on the defensive. Every conversation, email, or decision is tinged with the need to prove something. A huge chip on someone's shoulder can lead to a self-protective display of arrogance, an offensive stance to neutralize perceived attacks. What's interesting is that leaders with low self-worth have often "overachieved," and have ample reason to be confident rather than insecure, if only they could see themselves accurately.

4. LEARNED BEHAVIOR

People replicate what they've been exposed to, repeating behaviors that appeared successful in other settings. So if your friend began her career in a company culture where spiteful behavior was the norm, chances are she'll engage in that behavior herself as a reflex. If you know anyone who grew up in a family that thrived on dramatic emotional displays, then that's how they learned to express themselves. But in this instance, imitation is not a desirable form of flattery. It's a poison that needs to be identified and drained before it taints the rest of the environment.

5. FRUSTRATION

We all get frustrated now and then. When a plum assignment or promotion you've been hoping for goes to someone else, it's normal to be upset. But without self-awareness, the distance between frustration and anger is a short ride. That's often the case for people who feel they are trapped in disappointing situations at work or in their personal lives. Being unwilling to take responsibility for the outcomes in their lives, preferring to play the victim, can also fuel the fire of anger.

Expressions of anger: Eight signs to look for at home and at work

You know the conventional signs of anger. Voices rise. Veins bulge. A hand slams down on a table. But there's a huge difference between someone who gets angry occasionally and someone whose ongoing response is the nuclear option. By the time a chronically angry person reaches the boiling point, other things have been at work, early warnings that can help everyone decipher what's actually happening. Here are eight behaviors that both parties—people with anger and the people they afflict—can examine to see how ongoing anger expresses itself.

1. *Gotcha! Falling into a trap and justifying rage—in the angry person's eyes*
    In *The Games People Play*, his groundbreaking book about the psychological concept of Transactional Analysis, Eric Berne described a common form of anger as "Now I've Got You, You SOB." A typical "gotcha" is when someone has said or done something that gives the angry person reason to be upset—in their mind, anyway. But the punishment doesn't fit the crime. The infraction, the emotional equivalent of a breeze rustling leaves on a hill, has triggered an instant avalanche, almost as if someone has thrown a switch. In truth, this type of angry person is always waiting for an excuse to unleash their fury. Days, weeks or even years of pent-up anger bubble over without warning. This type of anger is particularly troubling because it makes people wielding it feel entitled, and often can convince everyone around him that they are. Don't be surprised if you catch a "gotcha" artist breaking into a smile after the "crime," delighted that someone's given them the license to erupt.

2. *Passive-aggressives show anger in ways you may not recognize*
    We know that passive-aggressive acts look benign on the surface, but are proxies for something more sinister. What may not be obvious to you is that passive-aggression is often the result of what we call a "HeadTrash Cocktail," a lethal blend of anger with a fear or control chaser. Passive-aggressive people are peeved, all right. But they're often too frightened or

manipulative to show it head on. So they express their hostility indirectly, with actions that speak far louder than their veiled words. Late arrivals, missed appointments, or inappropriate social or verbal actions may be the tip of a deep and dangerous iceberg. What's especially interesting about these people is that they themselves may not even recognize the root cause of their actions.

3. *LOUD gets out of trouble*

"Crazy has power." That brilliant observation comes from author, counselor, and motivational speaker John Bradshaw, who reminds us that people will use extreme behaviors to control situations. For example, on a crowded subway car, where every seat is taken, the person waving his hands and talking to himself out loud parts the crowd like Moses before the Red Sea, to reveal a seat with his name on it. Angry people know this, and in high stakes moments play the crazy card. "This kind of person will become big and loud to get out of a painful conversation. They raise their voice and make a scene, and you never get to the real issue," Tim says.

4. *Shuts down, then gets out of town*

A first cousin to Let's Get Loud is what we call Shut Down. As the name implies, the "aggrieved" party tries to gain the upper hand by ending the proceedings in the most definitive way possible. Think about how you felt having someone hang up on you, walk out abruptly during a heated conversation, or go silent in the middle of an email or text exchange. The effect is that the person terminating communication is in charge, deciding by physical imperative that the argument is over. You should have nothing more to say about it! Few things are more hostile than denying someone an opportunity to speak their peace after they've been yelled at. The Shut Down gives the person doing it a sense of control while taking cover. It's a power play, pure and simple.

5. *Going along to get along. Anything to stop the screaming*
Anger is a two-sided chemical reaction, a boiling pot that scalds the person dishing out the ire and the person receiving it. A clear signal that one party in a relationship has an anger habit is when the other party continually adjusts their responses to avoid a big blow up. "The phrase we use is 'Meeting the beast,' which means that people who are the target of habitual rage know they are going to be in the line of fire," says Tish. "So they constantly compromise to keep the peace. The pain is not worth the gain in their eyes."

6. *Avoiding whatever triggers the anger*
People who have to deal with bosses, colleagues, family members, or significant others who are frequently angry may become adept at dodging. There are topics, people, and whole categories of life they will avoid to keep from triggering a blowup. They rationalize that life is better when the other person isn't fulminating. What they don't realize, or want to accept, is that they've compartmentalized away whole parts of their existence for some peace and quiet.

7. *Doubting your values*
People who feel entitled to their rage are often adept at expressing their point of view, and equally skilled at crushing the reasonable arguments of others. Combine a perennially angry person with an insecure person, and before long the

weaker personality will likely begin to experience self-doubt. When a relationship makes you start to doubt what you stand for, it's time to ask whether you've compromised a part of your soul for a relationship that is damaging you.

8. *Very quiet—and seething inside*
Silence can be deadly. This type of anger is expressed through absence, where a person voices discontent by saying nothing. Everyone can be deceived into thinking the other person is fine, just being quiet or thoughtful, when in fact he or she is boiling over, all the while counting your sins and waiting to inflict the Big Payback. The less that is said, and the longer words are withheld, the more hostility they're dishing out. What they're not sharing, however, is anything you can use to begin a dialogue and mend that fence. Seethers are sponges, quietly absorbing their own bile.

A WORD OF CAUTION ABOUT ANGER: CALM DOWN, AND CONSIDER OUTSIDE HELP

Anger can reach regrettable extremes quickly, hitting a flash-point in an instant. Once you've identified anger as a HeadTrash of someone you care for or have to deal with, be vigilant. The moment you sense that things are getting out of hand, try to defuse the situation by calling for a time-out. Suggest taking up the conversation at another time, when both of you are ready to handle the discussion respectfully. Make sure the environment is safe before you continue the conversation.

One way to deal with conflicts that begin to escalate is to have a process in place that you've agreed to in advance. You may institute a "no shouting rule" or a "no insult policy," to prevent difficult discussions from going off the rails and getting worse.

Guidelines established before the war breaks out can help maintain civility, even while you're arguing.

However, when episodes repeat themselves and continue to intensify, it's important to consider seeking outside intervention. Never allow an exchange to become so heated that it becomes physical, or devolves into threats or insults that you'll later regret. "There's an expression that describes this perfectly: 'If it feels unhealthy, it is unhealthy.' Trust your instincts," Tim says. And when things get out of hand, take a break, or consider seeing an outside counselor.

Behind the Scenes with Tish and Tim: Anger Anecdote— Her politics versus their marriage

Tish's friend Bob was dating a woman, Carol, who was passionate in her opinions. "That was part of what attracted Bob to Carol. She was a real live wire," Tish said. "People found her either captivating or irritating, there was no middle ground."

Carol was always vocal about what she believed in, wearing it like a badge. Bob respected that, and their budding romance quickly led to cohabitation, and in turn to a second marriage for both of them.

Bob knew what he was getting into, or so he thought. In the beginning, his political differences with his new wife were simply divergent points of view that produced animated debates, with a few commonalities he sought to emphasize. He respected Carol's position and bent in her direction as much as he could. But over the years, as U.S. politics polarized and Carol found more like-minds on the Internet, her stances grew more extreme. She could no longer agree to disagree. Instead she increasingly insisted that her husband was simply and utterly wrong.

Carol became a popular blogger among people who agreed with her politics. Combined with troubled relationships with her adult children, this made her even more inflexible to opposing views. Tish says, "Carol came into the relationship with an anger problem. And it only got worse as her other close relationships began to break down. Eventually Carol's politics became her identity, and she began to see Bob's difference of opinion as personal rejection, more like an abandonment. There were deeper things going on here, with roots going back for decades. But the trunk of the tree was anger."

Bob suggested marriage counseling, but Carol was having none of it, holding her ground and her point of view. "Why should I give a therapist my money, when I know I'm right?" Finally, after fifteen years of marriage, and eight of screaming, she suggested a divorce, which Bob agreed to gladly.

An Anger Checklist and Comparison

HOW TO IDENTIFY ANGER HEADTRASH IN SOMEONE YOU KNOW.

ANGRY PEOPLE . . .	CALM PEOPLE . . .
Keep people on edge and guessing.	Are open and clear on big issues
Use fear to get what they want.	Gain trust, respect other viewpoints.
It's their way or the highway.	Encourage independent thought.
Have to have the final word.	Want to hear what you have to say.
Create an atmosphere of fear.	Want a safe environment.

(continued)

ANGRY PEOPLE . . .	CALM PEOPLE . . .
Oversee everything.	Delegate responsibility.
Can blow up relationships.	Help people thrive.
Stifle fresh thinking.	Inspire innovation.

HeadTrash Alert! A Quick Quiz on Anger

TO ASSESS WHETHER SOMEONE YOU KNOW HAS ANGER HEADTRASH, USE THE FOLLOWING QUIZ:

	Never	Sometimes	Often	Always
1. People try to say what this person wants to hear.				
2. Feels the need to "punish" those who get out of line.				
3. Believes it is necessary to yell in order to get a team to perform.				
4. When someone fails to produce, this person's first instinct is to get mad.				
5. Even family members get nervous around this person.				

(continued)

	Never	Sometimes	Often	Always
6. Always plays to win, even in small issues.				
7. After an outburst, this person will ask if it was an overreaction.				
8. Often has to apologize for displays of anger.				

If you checked "often" or "always" three or more times, the person in question probably has anger HeadTrash.

I (Tish) think anger is unique. It's not like other HeadTrashes. People can easily mistake insecurity for fear. Or arrogance for control. But anger is a one-off. It stands alone with its own behaviors. Once you define anger, you see it's a lone wolf. And people with anger may not recognize it because it's so deeply embedded in them.

Actually, I (Tim) have a caveat. Some people also confuse anger with control, but that's not accurate. People use anger to control others, but it's not the same. It's a cocktail. The HeadTrash of anger threatens and coerces. That looks like control, but the source is anger. It's so intense it makes people feel entitled to abuse others, but they'd never label it abuse.

The counterintuitive side of anger: Use it constructively

It sounds odd, but anger can actually be a force for good. After all, when you strip away the desire to do harm and quell the urge to lash out, what you're left with is energy, fuel you can use to motivate yourself. Harnessing the energy of anger can drive a person to achieve beyond their perceived limits, and overcome the barriers that others want to put around them. "Half of what I've achieved is because I didn't take no for an answer," says Tish. "I was angry that people tried to limit me. I had teachers tell me that I couldn't get into an Ivy League school, and bosses say I'd never start a business. I was driven to prove them wrong. Anger drove me forward, and made me stand up to my challenges." But it takes self-awareness to recognize the rage, and discipline to turn the negative impulses into forward motion.

ADVISING THE PERSON WITH THE HEADTRASH OF ANGER

Think of the nastiest, most despicable person you've ever met. Even that evil miscreant, who would as soon cut your heart out as say hello, loves someone or something, and probably has valued friends and relations. So that is where you start. When you're working with people whose HeadTrash is anger, begin by pointing out—respectfully and without blame—how their anger affects the people around them, especially the people who matter most to them. Suggest to them (or yourself if you're reading this for your own benefit) that their lives and the lives of the people they value will be better when they own their garbage and use the following tools to work with it.

CHANGE YOUR MIND, LITERALLY: THINK YOUR WAY OUT OF ANGER

Anger is the exhibitionist of HeadTrashes. The language is hyperbolic, the actions extreme. Anger-mongers scare with flair.

In the heat of the moment, they don't think twice about shouting "I'll kill him, that SOB," "I don't get mad; I get even," or "Just shoot me." They tell themselves that a bad event is "the worst thing that could ever happen." Such phrases demonstrate the violent, irrational thoughts that linger in a hostile mind. But if angry people can learn to stand back and look at their thoughts, and see how irrational they are, they can begin to control those thoughts and even replace them.

Common sense has a way of defusing explosive emotions, allowing us to stop thrashing and be more reasonable with our loved ones and ourselves. We may see that a bad situation is not really the apocalypse, and new words and emotions may begin to replace the dramatic ones. Even if calmer alternatives don't bubble up naturally, just looking at our thoughts gives us the opportunity to adjust our thinking and consciously substitute reasonable words for reflexive extremes.

PREPARATION REDUCES AGITATION AND INSTIGATION

The best way to deal with difficult topics is in person, or at the very least by phone. However, you don't want the angry person to see this as an opportunity to fight mano a mano. The goal is to resolve the conflict calmly, and figure out ways to move forward. Encourage the angry person to prepare for the meeting, and plan out your own questions and goals ahead of time. Pre-editing your language can also be helpful. Saying "You should have" or "Why didn't you" will trigger hostility and defensiveness. Instead ask, "What could we have done differently," "Where were the gaps," or "How can I help you resolve this?" And never doubt the power of asking, "Can you help me understand your thinking here?" Nonjudgmental phrases, spoken with sincerity, become a bridge to a more productive path.

ARE YOU PERFECT? IS ANYONE? REALITY, ANGER REDUCER 1

It's remarkable how we often hold people to a higher standard than ourselves. But if we're honest, we don't always live up to our own ideals, even when we set the bar low. And you won't be surprised to learn that the rest of the world is human, too. To save yourself or someone you're coaching from perennial bitterness, be realistic. People will behave in ways that surprise and disappoint us. They will drop the ball, misinterpret, or have their own priorities. Instead of holding a silent grudge, deal with issues before resentment builds. After both parties have shared their points of view, acknowledge what you heard, show your respect for their position, and then move on.

LAUGHTER, ANGER REDUCER 2

There's a reason people say, "Laughter is the best medicine." It has proven psychological and physical benefits. WebMD reported that a steady diet of funny can increase blood flow, improve immune response, lower blood sugar level, and aid sleep. Used wisely, humor can also quickly defuse anger, while shining a different light on the argument. Learning how to laugh at ourselves, versus taking ourselves so seriously, can be a huge relief to people we love and to us. Picture the outcome if we said, "I'm so angry! A rabbi, a priest, and a monkey walk into a bar . . . ." What's more, finding the humor in what we consider to be a hostile event can lessen the stress and allow us to see a more realistic picture.

AVOID IT TODAY. CONFRONT IT TOMORROW IN A CALMER STATE

At the very beginning of this chapter we said that everyone has their buttons, the things that set them off. The first responsibility that people with anger HeadTrash have is to know what really gets under their skins. Have the angry person do a trigger inventory to find out their flashpoints. That way they can begin to control their emotions when they confront one of their pet peeves.

Let the person you're helping know that time is the best balm for anger. Are they feeling their blood starting to boil? Point out that it's a good idea to wait for a calmer frame of mind before dealing with a teenager about a messy room, a spouse with an annoying habit, or a colleague who's pushing their buttons. Whatever their flashpoints are, angry people should know them and be alert to their first signs, so that their blood pressure doesn't rise any higher than it has to.

Remember, anger is often a spontaneous emotion, an eruption that may have been brewing but impels the person who has it to seek immediate resolution. So here's one of those rare moments where procrastination is actually a good thing. If you can help an angry person learn to put off explosions until tomorrow, you'll have done that person, and everyone he or she knows, a big favor. The explosions will grow smaller, and over time less frequent.

Arrogance—Looking Down on Others to Build Themselves Up

"There's no other way to say it. She's the most obnoxious person I've ever met. We had dinner with her and her husband, and no matter what we discussed, she dominated every conversation with long-winded rants on her points of view. She had opinions about everything and everyone. And she was going to share them whether I asked or not. My husband is very friendly with her husband, but I don't think we'll be seeing them for a while. A little bit of her goes a long way."

It's a shame that you're just not as smart as the person who suffers from the HeadTrash of arrogance. A pity, really, because you would be a far better human being if you were. Just ask that person, and he or she will tell you, and tell you, and tell you, until you're running for the door.

Suffering with a serious medical problem? The arrogant person will diagnose your symptoms, recommend medications, and then evaluate your doctors for you. Never mind that he's not a doctor himself. Just made some money in the stock market? Well, you could have made twice as much if only you'd consulted Ms. Arrogant Stock Wiz first, and then invested in some of her winners.

"I know you're the specialist, but if you can't
agree with me, I'll have to reject your diagnosis."

The funny thing is, sometimes the arrogant person actually is the smartest person in the room, which makes it that much more challenging to help them work through that character flaw. In any case it's hard to convince those who are certain they're the be-all and end-all to bring a little less of themselves to the table. Worse yet is that arrogance, like other HeadTrash traits, is often visible to everyone but the person who has it.

If you're planning to advise someone you think has the Head-Trash of arrogance, read the next few pages and be prepared. It may not be easy.

Case History: The attorney who tries everyone's patience at family gatherings

Weddings, communions, and bar mitzvahs. Special occasions that draw friends and family from far and wide to spend extended weekends talking, drinking, eating, and then repeating the process. As bonds are renewed, relatives hang out and sort out what's been happening in each other's lives since the last gathering. The clock slows down and the rest of the world disappears for a few days.

Cousins Joanie and Arlene were lovingly interrogating each other for every detail on how their children were doing. Harry, Joanie's high school junior, had begun visiting colleges.

"He's looking at liberal arts schools. So far we've been to SUNY Binghamton and Vassar," Joanie said. "Next week we're doing the expensive schools of New England tour—you know Brown, Harvard, Tufts, and Brandeis."

"Wow, that's some list," Arlene said.

"I know," Joan replied. "There may be a stretch school in there, but Harry has great grades. How can it hurt? We'll decide later which schools it makes sense to apply to."

"You know how it works at those colleges, right?" A third voice pushed its way into the conversation. It was Jenny, Arlene's sister in-law, the successful trial attorney. "Honey, you don't get into schools like that unless you know someone. Brown and Harvard? Oh, please. You better have an in."

"Jenny, he's in the top of his class," Joan replied.

"Come on, don't be naïve. Good grades and a clever essay are just the price of admission," Jenny countered. "Everyone has those. The rubber meets the road behind closed doors. That's where the administration decides who's at the table. And you better know people in that room, or your son's going to a public university like all the other yahoos. Now, I happen to know a provost at Brown. He's an old law-school buddy of mine. I'll make a call for you."

A smug grin on her face showed Jenny's self-satisfaction. She had won her favorite game of "I know it all." The lawyer had made her case and highlighted it by offering to introduce her unenlightened, less-connected cousin with someone from her rarefied stratum. Only Jenny knew how the world worked, and she was rubbing everyone's face in it, while appearing magnanimous. What she thought was benevolence, however, her cousins saw as nothing more than the rude haughtiness they had come to expect from her.

Arrogant as they want to be: Seven signs to look for at home and at work

You probably could have written some of this section yourself. Does anyone living or working with an arrogant person really need to be told the signs? We doubt it, but believe it or not, the person with that arrogance still needs to get a clue. He or she will benefit when you bring up these daily examples of their HeadTrash. That's because arrogant people are blind to that shortcoming. Oblivious! And if they are at all aware, what you see as an Achilles heel they feel is a strength. "Arrogant? I'm confident!" is a rationalization you'll hear a lot. A favorite quip of NBA great Charles Barkley is, "It ain't bragging if it's true." Sorry, Charlie, but it is bragging, and that's just one of the many distasteful faces of arrogance.

One last note: if someone you know exhibits the traits below, but you haven't identified them as arrogant, you may need to look at yourself first and ask why you're buying into their superiority complex. What causes you to identify this behavior as positive? What price are you paying for it in social isolation and lowered self-esteem? Arrogance unchecked affects everyone around, especially close family members and friends.

1. *Always ready to thump their chests.*
   Arrogant people don't need much to throw a parade for themselves. Any observation, any point won in a discussion, any achievement big or small is enough to send the confetti flying. They're ready to roar at the slightest confirmation of their own worth, or any threat to it. "Boast" is their default setting. "What a jerk" is often the reaction to it.

2. *Always the brightest bulb in the candelabrum.*
   Charles Darwin called it "natural selection." Herbert Spencer later described it as "survival of the fittest." The concept is that that in any group, there will always be someone who is the "fittest," or for our purposes, the smartest or most evolved. And that will always be the arrogant person, in his or her own mind, anyway. Their thoughts are not just opinions. They are facts! Insights! Pearls of wisdom! The reality is that many people with the HeadTrash of arrogance really are quite bright. But their insistence that everyone know it lowers the perceived value of what they have to say. Before people actually hear an arrogant colleague, friend, or family member utter a word, they first hear themselves thinking, "Oh, no. Here we go again."

3. *When relating to others, they're condescending.*
   When arrogant people finally deign to look in your direction,

chances are they're looking down. They're patronizing, their words and actions giving off a holier- and brainier-than-thou air. A big clue is how they interact with others. Usually, they don't. They simply tolerate other people, unless it's someone they have a need for or—a rare occurrence indeed—someone they think is on their level.

4. *They don't need your opinions. They have their own.*
   Looking for consensus? Eager to build a team ethos? Don't bother looking here. Why would the person who knows everything need to hear from you? She's had all it figured out from the day she was born. No wonder arrogant people typically do poorly in group settings, or being part of a team. If they're not running the show, or the consigliere to the person who is, they're just not happy. And you'll know about it.

5. *They're bad listeners.*
   It's not surprising that people with strong opinions don't do well hearing yours. Not only do they cherish their own point of view; they're emotionally unequipped to listen patiently to what anyone else has to say. Their ears hear only the thoughts forming in their own heads, blocking out your point of view before you've finished expressing it. Does that sound narcissistic? It should because it is, and that's a big part of the problem (more on that later).

6. *They're dismissive of other people.*
   When you believe that you're royalty, everyone else becomes "the little people," easily disdained and diminished. Tone is everything, and the tone of the arrogant person oozes haughty superiority. She brushes aside everyone else's needs and thoughts. If she ever considered them in the first place.

7. *Their social circle is more like a dot.*

Whether they know it or not, arrogant people are destined to be anti-social. Perhaps it's because so few people in their estimation are worthy of their time. People who spend their time devaluing and dismissing everything in advance leave little room for new relationships. Or perhaps it's because so few people can stand being with them for any length of time. If you're living or working with an opinionated person, whose circle of friends you can count on one hand, you're looking at arrogance in action.

Behind the Scenes with Tish & Tim: Arrogance Anecdote—The entitled in-laws

Gus and Danielle never looked forward to visits from Danielle's sister Meg and her husband, Hank. Meg and Hank had compiled a long and consistent scorecard of frustrating everyone around them. That they would arrive late was a given, so predictable that Danielle had taken to padding all arrival times by an hour to keep them nearly on schedule. But Danielle couldn't forgive herself if she didn't invite Meg and Hank on important occasions.

At every meal, Hank expected to be waited on like a pasha. Gus told Tim in exasperation one day, "His audacity amazes me. If something is missing at a meal, God forbid he hauls his butt out of the chair. Instead he barks, 'Danielle, can you get the salt?' It drives me nuts!"

The most recent offense had occurred when the family was at the dinner table, wondering when Meg and Hank would come downstairs. Of course they were running late, but this time they were actually in the house, in the guest room! Ten minutes passed. Then twenty minutes, then twenty-five. Gus said, "I already had a button on me about this, so I was ready to charge up the stairs and bust down the door. But Danielle offered to go to keep the peace."

She disappeared up the steps, and returned in a few minutes, an astonished look on her face. "Okay, you're not going to believe this. They're in the middle of watching a movie," she said.

"It's 6:30," Gus said. "What movie is on TV now?"

"The one they rented on demand," Danielle replied. "They said we should eat without them."

Gus told Tim, "They knew we were waiting, and they not only ignored dinner, they rented a movie on our cable TV account. With our money! Without asking us! What makes people think they can do that?"

In a word, arrogance. Tim says, "I told my friend that his in-laws have a profound sense of entitlement. That leads them to believe that common courtesies don't apply. And that everyone else should accommodate their wishes." Call it rude, selfish, or thoughtless. The root of it is arrogance.

Confidence or insecurity? What is the source?

Many arrogant people behave like an answer in search of a question. They enter any situation knowing it all, primed to unravel all the riddles of your world. They're so quick to comment confidently, it's easy to be persuaded of their incomparable brilliance. And sometimes the arrogant person truly is brilliant. But whether or not the arrogant person has above-average smarts, arrogance is really a mask that prevents outsiders from seeing the insecurity inside. People who create ways to boast about their achievements without being asked, who are all too willing to brag about how much money they're making or the new car they're driving, are hiding poor self-worth under a sheen of fake self-esteem. Before you offer advice to the person with the HeadTrash of arrogance, it's helpful to step back to see what you're dealing with. And then proceed with caution.

Penny's Perspective

People who are truly confident and competent (versus arrogant) rarely brag about their knowledge or skills. The most successful people exude a sense of quiet self-confidence and modesty. They often follow the philosophy that everyone has something to teach them, and listen to others with respect. I remember seeing another consultant who was with a mutual high-end prospect in Dubai. During his meeting he proceeded to puff out his chest and speak loudly. After the consultant left, the prospect told me that this man must not be very confident, because his insecurity was speaking loud and clear.

An Arrogance Checklist and Comparison

HOW TO IDENTIFY ARROGANCE HEADTRASH IN SOMEONE YOU KNOW.

ARROGANT PEOPLE . . .	CONFIDENT PEOPLE . . .
Are self-centered. Pretend to be interested in you, but really care only about themselves.	Consider others in their actions and want to help them do well, too.
Are solo operators. Never invite or welcome useful advice and help.	Are modest and open to alternate opinions. Often ask, *"What do you think?"*

(continued)

ARROGANT PEOPLE ...	CONFIDENT PEOPLE ...
Get insulted and feel threatened easily. Their way is the best way, the only way!	Seek out other people's good ideas and are eager to endorse them, without needing credit.
In the guise of wanting feedback are just looking for pats on the back.	In an effort to improve, ask for constructive criticism.
Want power for prestige and control over others.	Pursue leadership roles to contribute to the greater good.
Use people to fulfill their own needs. See others as means to an end.	Sincerely care for others.
Pontificate. Dominate meetings and family gatherings with their opinions.	Listen to others, and speak up only when they have something useful to say.

A clinical definition that might be helpful

Scan the list below, and see if a few of these traits ring a bell:

- An exaggerated sense of one's own abilities and achievements

- A constant need for attention, affirmation, and praise

- A belief that he or she is unique or "special" and should only associate with other people of the same status

- Persistent fantasies about attaining success and power

- Exploiting other people for personal gain

- A sense of entitlement and expectation of special treatment

- A preoccupation with power or success

- Feeling envious of others, or believing that others are envious of him or her

- A lack of empathy for others

Although the bullet points above sound like raging arrogance, they are actually the clinical symptoms of Narcissistic Personality Disorder, as identified by the *Diagnostic and Statistical Manual of Mental Disorders* (DSM-5), published by the American Psychiatric Association. The Mayo Clinic says, "If you have narcissistic personality disorder, you may come across as conceited, boastful or pretentious. You often monopolize conversations. You may belittle or look down on people you perceive as inferior. You may feel a sense of entitlement—and when you don't receive special treatment, you may become impatient or angry. You may insist on having 'the best' of everything—for instance, the best car, athletic club or medical care."

Sound familiar? Then that should be telling. People with arrogance are narcissists, albeit perhaps not to the degree where they mirror each and every ill conceit mentioned here. But it's worth remembering that most are so self-focused that they're unable to understand, let alone see, why anyone would be offended by their vision of the world. They would counter, "After all, isn't it the truth?" To them, it is. Thus contributing to what we call "The Arrogance Blind Spot."

Combine arrogance with charisma, and the blind spot can enlarge to include many other people. It's not unusual for someone with arrogance HeadTrash to adopt a persona of noble self-sacrifice, which then excuses otherwise inexcusable actions.

Think of the cult leader who sexually abuses disciples or rips them off financially, or the politician whose real agenda is not public service but personal power. But religion and politics don't have a monopoly on arrogance HeadTrash by any means. Every arena has its share of people on missions of self-aggrandizement masquerading as noble leadership.

When someone believes his point of view is true, and is too narcissistic to see beyond his own nose and needs, he's incapable of comprehending his actions as anything but accurate and supportive.

HeadTrash Alert! A Quick Quiz on Arrogance

TO ASSESS WHETHER SOMEONE YOU KNOW HAS ARROGANCE HEADTRASH, USE THE FOLLOWING QUIZ:

	Never	Sometimes	Often	Always
1. Behaves as if nothing moves forward without them.				
2. Always has trouble admitting an error or fault.				
3. Is avoided by those needing counsel.				
4. Wants to run the show every time and feels no one else is able to.				
5. Rejects, attacks, or twists other people's ideas to dominate the situation.				

(continued)

	Never	Sometimes	Often	Always
6. Interrupts others or cuts them out of conversations entirely.				
7. Rarely compromises for the greater good of the group.				

If you checked "often" or "always" three or more times, the person in question probably has arrogance HeadTrash.

People ask me (Tim) how they can tell the difference between confidence and arrogance. The sign is whether you enjoy the person. Pure arrogance is impossible to be around. But a little arrogance that comes from knowing your stuff and being sure of yourself is okay. It's the person who's unaware of how his or her behavior infuriates others who is hard to swallow.

I (Tish) agree. People with arrogance are terrible listeners. It's as if they have no social skills. They're unable to respect anyone else's view. They only value their own side of the story. They come across as selfish. The challenge is when they can't separate knowing their stuff from not listening. You may be the smartest person in the room, but you don't have to prove it every time.

Advising the person with the HeadTrash of arrogance

Oh, you brave soul. Your job is to counsel a condescending know-it-all on how to be a better person, on how to cultivate some humility and demonstrate humanity. This with a person who could cut you in half.

Whoever the arrogant person is—family member, friend, boss, colleague, or employee—you have probably spent a fair amount of time ignoring their offenses to give yourself a breather. But that only lasts so long because they demand too much attention, and they're part of your life, like it or not. So here are some tools to help you effectively advise the arrogant person in your life.

FIND THE RIGHT TIME

It's tempting to want to seize the moment, to catch an arrogant person in the act of being El Supremo and then blurt out, "This is exactly what I'm talking about. You're being a jerk!" Tempting yes, but also counterproductive. When arrogant people are saddled up on their high horses, you'll never knock them down. And it makes you look almost as bad as the person you're hoping to help. Much better to wait for a quiet moment, when the arrogant person's superiority complex may have relaxed a bit. And when you do broach the topic of that person's arrogance, avoid being confrontational. Instead of making "the talk" an accusation, make it a conversation. You may even want to schedule it in advance, to give that person fair warning that it's coming.

No matter how you slice it, you may be wrong in that person's eyes. After all, he or she does know everything. But you want to show the same respect you hope they'll finally show the other people in their life.

DON'T TAKE THE BAIT, DON'T DEBATE

Good luck trying to win a heated argument with the arrogant person. You can't, and that's not your goal here. Your objective is to help this person see how their actions and words are hurting others, and ultimately undermining themselves as well. When that conversation becomes a battle, it's easy to lose your composure, especially when the scornful, nasty comments fly. Score a point for arrogance. Instead, don't be afraid to calmly say, "Let me finish, you'll have your chance to speak when I'm done." Don't get into an insult fest or a my-facts-are-truthier-than-yours exchange. Keep it cool.

IF NECESSARY, CALL FOR A TIME OUT

Even though you may have the best intentions, and the serenity of a Zen monk, things can get out of hand quickly. One reason is that arrogant people just don't back down. Another is that they're sensitive to being criticized. So before people begin saying too many things they'll regret later on, call for a time out, ASAP. "Create some space and be willing to step away," says Tim. "This gives the other person time to reflect on what you've been saying away from the heat of the moment."

CONSIDER BRINGING IN A THIRD PARTY TO MEDIATE

As we've said, when the person you want to help has an extreme case of HeadTrash it can be beneficial to have an impartial third party handle the discussion with you. If you feel uncertain about talking to a person with arrogance HeadTrash, consider bringing in a psychologist, mediator, or personal coach. There's no guarantee that the arrogant person will be any more receptive to taking feedback from a third party, but it may add some objectivity to the discussion. At the very least, it takes you off of the hot seat.

ARROGANCE: AN EXCERPT
FROM OUR FIRST HEADTRASH BOOK

Share this with the person who has the HeadTrash of arrogance

Sometimes the best way to guide someone to a better path is by letting them find it on their own. Instead of trying to pound your point of view into his head, share this section with the person you want to help. Here are six tips and tools, taken from our first book, *HeadTrash: Cleaning Out the Junk that Stands Between You and Success.*

1. CULTIVATE HUMILITY.

Arrogant leaders tend to think of humility as weak. That's a false perception. Humility means being realistic about yourself, your ideas and your abilities. It means being honest enough to accept your limitations and admit that you're not perfect. You acknowledge that you can—and do—make mistakes.

At its core, humility is about truth. If you want to move forward, you need to be firmly rooted in the truth.

Business experts around the world have embraced this principle. The late C.K. Prahalad, who was a globally respected corporate strategy and management expert, asserted, "Leadership is self-awareness, recognizing your failings, and developing modesty, humility and humanity." Jim Collins, bestselling author of *Good to Great*, puts humility at the core of what he calls "Level 5 Leadership." Collins says of humble leaders: "They routinely credit others, external factors, and good luck for their companies' success. But when results are poor, they blame themselves. They also act quietly, calmly, and determinedly—relying on inspired standards, not inspiring charisma, to motivate."

2. ACKNOWLEDGE AND APOLOGIZE.

If your arrogance has resulted in words or actions that have hurt or put down others, you need to openly acknowledge your inappropriate behavior and apologize for it. Failing to do so and simply attempting to "be nice to everybody" looks phony. Few people will believe you, and the rest will wonder what you're up to. Plus, it will be easy for you to slip back into old patterns at the first provocation.

But a public acknowledgment carries with it a commitment to follow through. It gives you a needed impetus to change your behavior. It also gives people a framework in which to understand and react to your change.

You don't necessarily have to say, "I'm sorry" (though there are no more powerful words in the English language). Try such phrases as "That wasn't my intent," or "I didn't realize my actions had that kind of impact; I only want the best for all of us." You—and your co-workers or employees—can then move on.

Saying "I'm sorry" is a stumbling block for many leaders who have been raised in the "no excuses" school. Perhaps the all-time example of this occurs in the great John Ford western *Fort Apache,* where the veteran cavalry officer played by John Wayne blisters a young lieutenant for a mistake and then tells him, "Don't apologize. It's a sign of weakness."

With all respect for John Ford and John Wayne (we both love the movies they made, separately and together), nothing could be further from the truth. Saying, "I'm sorry" and playing the victim, asking for pity—sure, that's a sign of weakness. But owning up to mistakes and apologizing for hurting other people for no good reason—that's a sign of strength. Great leaders know the difference and act accordingly.

3. BE CLEAR ABOUT WHAT YOU ARE GOING TO CHANGE.

Sustaining a behavioral change is tough. But it's easier if you're clear and specific right at the start about what you're planning to do differently. And don't keep that information to yourself! Let your peers and staff know about your goals.

Being explicit sets the standard for you personally, and gives your co-workers a solid basis for providing feedback. Like it or not, you will need feedback if you are really going to change. Although it may often result in a painful "ouch," you must both *solicit* and *accept* the comments of others. That means not jumping down someone's throat the first time they call you on your arrogant behavior. Or the second time. Or the third.

Instead, thank the person for their input. Don't justify yourself or try to rationalize. Simply accept the feedback and, as Walt Disney said, "Keep moving forward!" If you are consistent, you'll be saying "ouch" less and less as time goes on.

4. INVITE INPUT FROM OTHERS.

Arrogance is a very close-minded attitude. To change, you'll need to:

• Be open to ideas.

• Let people express their opinions.

- Become more approachable.

- Listen more.

- Talk less.

- Invite other people's contributions.

- Ask questions, and then let the other person talk.

- Put the other person first.

Life isn't all about you, and the best ideas don't all come from you. It's time to get out of your own way, and everyone else's, and open up to what others have to offer.

5. EMPOWER YOUR PEOPLE.

Let go! Stop controlling everything and give your people back their autonomy. Allow them to do the jobs you brought them in to do. Remember, you hired A-players for a reason. They have skills, talents, and experience your company needs. So cut them loose!

This doesn't mean that you never intervene or give advice. But you will need to move from *telling* people how to do their jobs to *coaching* them in their jobs. Telling is dictatorial. Coaching leads and guides people, but doesn't put them in a straitjacket.

And remember, people have their own styles and methods. A person's approach may be different than yours. But that doesn't make either approach better or worse, as long as the job gets done and gets done well. Besides, who wants a bunch of clones in the office? There is strength in diversity; there is power in differences.

So lighten up, loosen up, and empower your people. You'll find you have a lot fewer headaches when you do!

6. GIVE CREDIT WHERE CREDIT IS DUE.

One last piece of incredibly important advice: give credit where it's due! Recognize people's accomplishments. When someone comes up with a brilliant idea, acknowledge it—right then and there in public! Hand out rewards liberally: verbal affirmations, awards, promotions, recognition, etc.

Step out of the limelight. Let other people take their bows. And be sure to add your own applause.

Control—Always in Charge, in All Ways

"Her agenda is the only agenda. It doesn't matter what anyone else says. She just expects people to get "get with the program" because she said so. She makes every decision. I never feel like my point of view is considered, even though she's my wife."

People don't add the word "freak" to labels casually. We all know someone others describe as a *strict vegetarian* or *a total carnivore,* someone who's *extroverted,* or someone who's *shy.* But to get to the level of *freak,* well, that takes some effort, a type of energy that is exceptional, a devotion to your cause that inspires people to change your title. You have to earn "Control Freak." And those who do, come by it honestly.

Few decisions are too small to escape the management of the person suffering with the HeadTrash of Control, no task or mission that won't—in their estimation—benefit from their personal oversight. Starting to ponder whether to repaint a room in your house? She already has color chips in hand, with checks next to her favorite hues. Discussing where to have dinner? He arrives with "suggestions" that just happen to be on his personal top five list. *Relax, sit back, Buddy; I've got this,* control freaks telegraph. They have the answer. "With that type of person, it's not a conversation," says Tish. "You never get asked; you're always told."

"Harvard called. My spelling quiz will have no effect
on their admissions decisions 10 years from now."

Sure, it's helpful when someone takes the lead, when one person in the family or the office manages the minutiae and pushes things to completion. That's what effective individuals do. "But it crosses the line when it becomes a one-way street, when people stop having dialogue about the issues," says Tim. "Guidance and management should never be confused with control. They can look similar, but they are very different."

Case History: Personal misconduct at home, the sit and run

She's the marvel of your social circle, an accomplished architect who, while running a thriving firm, also manages to be an omnipresent mother. She (or maybe it's her clone) is somehow able to appear at a building construction site early in the morning, then work all day at the office, and then show up perfectly coiffed at the parent teacher event later that evening. All while sitting on a charity board or two. She makes everyone who knows her feel merely human or worse.

Because your tween-age daughter is in the same class at school as hers, the four of you recently became friendly. So it wasn't totally surprising when you got an email inviting the two of you to hang out at their swim club with them on the next day. "Plan to be there around 2:00," the note read. "Just wear your bathing suits, and bring your towels and your smiles!" It seemed a little late in the day to start a pool outing, but you didn't ask. You'd have lunch at home first.

When you arrived, *quelle surprise*! You weren't the only people invited. Two other moms and their daughters were already in attendance, and it felt like you were late to the party. In fact, in talking to the others, you learn that they had been invited for a poolside lunch ninety minutes earlier. What's more, these two girls were better friends with the architect's daughter than your own daughter was. It was uncomfortable, but here you were, and so you tried to make the best of it.

The afternoon progressed—the cool water and some ice cream working their magic and easing the initial discomfort. It wasn't long before everyone was talking and splashing around the pool.

Just as you were beginning to unwind, Superwoman said, "Oh my, look at the time! We'd better start wrapping up." It was only 4:00. Uncomfortable had now progressed to full-on awkward, a pall settling in as you folded towels and scooped up flip flops. *What's the rush,* you wondered? In the parking lot, you thanked your hostess for inviting you. She gave you a big hug. "This was lovely! We'll have to do it again!" she said, slamming her SUV door and burning rubber before you could respond.

After your daughter came home from school on Monday, she reported that Saturday night after the pool party the architect and her daughter had gone to see the hottest "tween idol" boy band with yet another girl, the real best friend of the architect's daughter, and the friend's mother. The 4:00 curfew was to leave time for dinner and getting dressed up for a 7:30 show.

What appeared to be a gracious act was in fact a master maneuver, a social scam run by a five-star control freak. Super Mom slotted *your* daughter in to fill a brief void in *her* daughter's life. The pool party was simply the bait, while you were an accessory. Control freaks, you see, will find ways to get their way, often gift-wrapping their true intentions.

Penny's Perspective

One of the key measures of our personal flexibility is our internal set of "rules and boundaries." Whether we know it or not, we each have a methodology that regulates how we play the game of life. We use our methodology to stay safe and adhere to positive behaviors.

Control freaks have an overzealous internal law enforcement code. When people don't follow their rules, they add more rules over time, losing sight of the big picture. And that only frustrates them and the people they have to live with every day.

In control to run or ruin the show: Five signs to look for at home and at work

Because the stereotype is obvious, everyone thinks they know how a controlling person behaves. But in addition to the in-your-face my-way-or-the-highway employer or family member, there are many other types of controlling personalities, and many ways for them to run your life, overtly or covertly.

1. *The Subtle Control Freak: empowering you to do exactly what they want*
   Beware the domineering person who says, "This is your deal. Go for it!" Sometimes you can see them magnanimously bestowing an opportunity with the left hand, while scribbling out every detail about what should be done with the right. But the Subtle CF can also be a passive-aggressive orchestrator who actually appears to be sharing responsibility. You feel like you really have a mission and a say in how to get there.

   Unfortunately, this type of control freak is often a manipulator, pulling the marionette strings behind the scenes. Watch out when family members or staffers you thought had nothing to do with the situation start asking you how it's going or weighing in with suggestions. Be equally alert when parts of the assignment move forward without your knowledge. Suspect directives that come from an invisible source. The Subtle CF talks a good game, but can't really let go long enough to let you have it your way.

2. *The Micromanager Control Freak: The devil is in your details*
You know this person's game, because there's nothing subtle about it. The Micromanager CF lets you know, step by step, inch by inch, exactly how he wants it done—even when he should have little say in the matter. At the office, these people often excel as project directors, account supervisors, and COOs. They get things done, all the while rubbing wrong the people who have to work with them.

As parents, they tend to be authoritarians who issue commands versus offering suggestions. And that pedantic behavior travels up the family food chain, too, goading spouses and siblings into doing their bidding. "There can be a know-it-all quality to their style, which they validate with their competence at handling the details," says Tish. But the bad easily outweighs the good when everyone around them begins feeling demeaned and diminished, while the Micromanager CF expresses his or her superiority complex, imaginary clipboard in hand.

3. *The Knowledge Hoarder Control Freak*
If knowledge is power, the Hoarder CF is not sharing any willingly.

At home, he may be the czar of the family finances, begrudgingly dispensing information only as it suits his needs, dismissing questions with statements like "It's too complicated to explain. You wouldn't understand." To maintain his status, he might spring a pop quiz, asking questions about something the rest of the family has limited background on.

At work, she maneuvers data and details like a chess master, mentally managing the for-public-consumption file against the rest of the information. Worse, she'll parse out pieces of data, so that no one person has all the facts to make an informed decision. If you find yourself arguing with a co-worker over an assignment, and the two of you have different takes on the details, you've been info-hoarded. Data chess keeps the knowledge-hoarding Control Freak secure in her domain and your ignorance.

4. *The By-the-Book Control Freak*
With apologies to your mother, the most powerful words in the English language are not "please and thank you." In the view of a by-the-book CF, the words that carry the most clout are *"According to."* How many times have you been pushed into a corner with "According to," followed by the name of a leading expert? In business, this person uses otherwise effective quality control tools such as Six Sigma and ISO 9000 like weapons, brandishing them in offensive strikes to get her way. We've witnessed leaders use management systems to maintain a tyrannical environment. Eventually, the office may run according to the system, but the tradeoffs show up when team members stop thinking and acting independently.

"Rigid control systems have a detrimental effect on staff. People just wait to be told what to do, or do just enough to satisfy the methodology," Tim says. Some will learn how to game the system, turning in all their sales just under the deadline, for example, or looking only for sales that are weighted higher.

At home, a family member will read a book and immediately become an authority on parenting or family dynamics, using her knowledge to keep everyone else in line. Information is a good thing, of course, but a by-the-book CF inflicts information overload to become information overlord. And everyone around the kitchen table now answers to "According to."

5. *The Legacy Control Freak: This is how we (our religion/our family/our company) always do it.*

    If you really want to control someone, co-opt a tradition. The Legacy CF knows that, and uses it effectively. Whole lives are ruled this way, from the moment children are born until they fulfill their destiny, in the legacy CF's eyes, by entering the family business. It's just understood that one day, some day, they will abandon their own passions and take the reins, even if they have no interest at all. The tools in the legacy toolbox may include referencing religion, heritage, or precedent. Of course there is also the HeadTrash of guilt at work here, too, creating a bitter HeadTrash cocktail.

    "I had a client who had gotten his MBA and was making his way in a Fortune 500 company," says Tish. "He was on a fast track. But his father called and said, 'It's time for you to come into the company,' and that was that. He was enjoying what he was doing, and he was successful. But the expectation was so strong, and his dad was so controlling, that he just did as he was told."

Behind the Scenes with Tish & Tim: Control Anecdote— The overpowering traveler

People who are "natural-born leaders" often have control issues. As a result, they can be difficult for peers to influence. Tish worked with a client, Bob, who served in the military as a junior officer and then got his MBA from the University of Chicago's Booth School of Business.

Bob loved his time in Chicago and was always looking for excuses to visit after he and his wife Mary moved back to Philadelphia. So when he heard that his buddy Joe was going to Chicago on business, he suggested tacking on a few days for a couples' weekend. "I offered to handle all the arrangements, because no one knows Chicago like I do," Bob said. It was exactly what Tish expected from her client.

"Bob is a classic take-charge guy. That serves him well much of the time," says Tish. The problem is when this personality type "can't gauge where taking charge stops and taking control begins."

After arriving at the hotel, the couples agreed to meet in 30 minutes. When Joe and Sue stepped off the elevator on schedule, Bob and Mary were already waiting in the lobby. "So, what do we have in mind tonight?" Sue said. "Maybe we can make a reservation before we leave."

Bob had already taken care of it. He informed everyone that they had a reservation at India House. The silence was deafening. Joe said, "Sue doesn't eat Indian food."

"That's why I picked India House," Bob said. "They have a broad menu, including some American dishes. I'm sure Sue will find something she likes."

Sue graciously said it was fine, and off they went. Even though it was 15-degrees colder than Philadelphia, Bob had decided they should walk so he could show them the sights. He had a special route planned.

"I took them down the main street of the Chicago Marathon, which I ran twice," Bob told Tish. Along the way, he pointed out a Thai restaurant where he once met a few of the Chicago Cubs. Two blocks later, they were in Wrigleyville, named for Wrigley Field. By now, they had trekked six blocks, and Bob was oblivious to everyone else's shivering. "How much farther are we going?" Joe asked.

"It's no more than two miles," Bob said.

"Two miles?" Sue blurted out. "Why don't we grab a cab? It's cold."

"That's no way to see this city," Bob said. "We'll be there in 20 minutes tops, if we hustle." It was becoming clear to everyone that this "tour" of Chicago was not for the benefit of the group, but to feed Bob's enormous need for control over how they saw Chicago.

Then someone shouted, "Bob, I'm freezing!" It was his wife, talking in her don't-mess-with-me voice. As Bob told Tish, "My wife said, 'I'm taking the first cab I see. If you insist on walking, we'll meet you at India House.' Then she turned her back on me and stuck her arm in the air."

Welcome to Chicago.

Over time, we helped Bob appreciate the impact of his controlling behavior on others. He came to see how rigid he could be and how barking orders in civilian life is not very effective. "Not everybody will obey your orders," Tish told him, "They have freedom of choice. Especially your wife."

Good control versus bad control: not knowing when to let go.

What CEO, family matriarch, or religious leader doesn't prefer some control? What leader doesn't want some stability and pre-dictability, the feeling that he or she has a firm grip on what's happening and what's coming next. And although it's in the leader's best interest to lessen chaos, control can be as good for the infantry as it is for the generals.

Any teacher worth their chalk knows that students do better when they have a sense of structure. They thrive on understand-ing what's expected of them and when. Businesses are not much different. Providing structure is important for all employees to perform at their best.

Is it any wonder that many people want to keep a tight grip on the wheel, want to be able to steer and veer with every detail? Control done well can lead to success: burgeoning businesses, thriving families, expanding congregations. The well-managed company adds new products and services. Children grow up, leave the nest, but stay connected and then add spouses and families of their own. The congregation, outgrowing its homey first church, gathers the board to vote on a capital campaign to build a larger space.

And that's when the moment of truth arrives, and organiza-tions learn whether their leaders can survive their own success. Control freaks continue to think they can manage everything on their own, but feeling the stress of added responsibilities they often shorten the leash on their reports. The result, says Tim, is that "the people under them become resentful. They feel like they're being punished for their success, being stifled because the leader wants to hem them in. Or they get in line and become compliant, like robotic zombies." Neither option allows an organization to build on its good fortune and move to the next level.

AN EXCERPT FROM OUR FIRST HEADTRASH BOOK

Share this section on how to deal with control

Juggling China versus Juggling Tupperware

When you have a lot of things on your plate, you have to prioritize. Here's an approach to beginning the process we call the china versus Tupperware test. Some issues are Tupperware challenges. If you juggle Tupperware and it falls, you or someone else can still pick it up and keep moving. It may be a little dented, or it may survive the fall without any damage. Either way, you haven't lost anything.

Under these guidelines, that assignment can be delegated.

Conversely, if you have good china and you drop it, it shatters, and it's gone, baby, gone. Those initiatives you probably want to handle yourself, or delegate to one of your superstars.

Control freaks believe that *everything* is fine china; *everything* is urgent and essential and can only be handled by one person. (Guess who?)

When every project and decision is a here-and-now crisis, long-term thinking vanishes. Without clear direction and a plan, you and your staff are either all over the place or stuck in crisis mode.

You fail and the company falters.

If there are 15 things on your to-do list, surely not all of them rise to china-level concern. Decide which tasks you truly can delegate. Then call those Tupperware, and act accordingly.

A Control Checklist and Comparison

HOW TO IDENTIFY CONTROL HEADTRASH IN SOMEONE YOU KNOW.

CONTROLLING PEOPLE . . .	EMPOWERING PEOPLE . . .
Monitor everyone and everything.	Allow people space to grow.
Suppress new ideas.	Encourage fresh thinking.
Dictate.	Suggest.
Put their interests ahead of the group.	Help the company flourish.
Keep people in the dark.	Are transparent and forthcoming.
Hold people back.	Urge people on.
Expect compliance.	Inspire commitment.
Instill fear.	Make everyone feel safe and respected.

HeadTrash Alert! A Quick Quiz on Control

TO ASSESS WHETHER SOMEONE YOU KNOW HAS CONTROL HEADTRASH, USE THE FOLLOWING QUIZ:

	Never	Sometimes	Often	Always
1. Struggles to let people make their own decisions without oversight.				
2. Delegates projects, but expects to be involved in their implementation.				
3. Makes people feel squeamish about asking for added direction on a project.				
4. Participates in all meetings and calls to ensure that the right decisions are made.				
5. Spends too much time correcting everyone else's work.				
6. Requires status updates before the agreed project benchmarks.				
7. Won't delegate highly visible assignments to someone else.				

What I (Tish) often see in controlling relationships is the "controlled" person" begins fighting with the controller. He becomes resentful and combative. But eventually he stops, because he realizes his opinions don't matter. He stops even expressing himself. He loses his sense of identity because it feels like he doesn't matter. It can be very demotivating.

Agreed. I (Tim) watch people become defeated. They think this is the way it is, so they become lifeless and sad. They have nothing to be excited about. But the other thing I see is that some people rebel. When they fight back, they fight dirty. They might undermine the other person, or do something behind their back because they don't feel they can face them directly. But that's exactly what they need to do. Find a way to constructively confront.

If you checked "often" or "always" three or more times, the person in question probably has control HeadTrash.

Advising the person with the HeadTrash of control

Before you begin, remember this: the person you're about to coach often *is* the coach. She sees herself as the person in charge. She may very well be, whether she's running the company, managing the department or heading the family. So she may not take kindly to the idea that you've been keeping score and have a different point of view on how she can manage her life and the people around her more effectively. You may want to consider partnering with others in your family or on your office staff before confronting this person, or bringing in a therapist or executive coach.

If you do decide to proceed, keep in mind that the control freak may be quite good at what he or she does. Many an effective team has a killer controller at the center of it, keeping all the plates in the air. Their awareness of their skills, and how they contribute to the success of their organizations, may make them less likely to embrace what you have to say. Come prepared.

When you confront a controlling person, be clear, firm, detailed, and calm. Anticipate a few fireworks, ranging from defensive postures to fact-filled justifications to outright bullying to put you in your place. Who are you, after all, to suggest that the person who's holding everything together has some flaws to work on?

That's a question you'll want to have the answer for, and the gist of it is this. Your counsel is not an attempt to undermine anyone's authority. It is not a power play, and it's not about you. Your goal is to enable the person with control HeadTrash to do a job better by pointing out opportunities for improvement. In fact, the end result is that they might be happier when they learn how to delegate more and lessen their stress.

DISARM WITH CHARM. BEGIN WITH POSITIVES AND APPRECIATION FOR THEIR EFFORTS AND SUPPORT

Sure it's one of the oldest rules in communication, and there's a reason why. It's much easier for anyone to hear criticism when you've first shown concern and admiration. You create an opening, which tells the other person you're not here to tear him or her down.

Remember you're talking to a control freak, a person who, before you know it, will have spun the conversation around and have you wondering about your own issues. Start by building a bridge you can both stand on as you begin a difficult conversation. A good way to do that is to own your piece of the issues. Are you sometimes a procrastinator, in need of a shove occasionally? Say so. It indicates that you recognize your flaws, too.

ASK OUT LOUD, "WHAT CAN YOU DELEGATE OR SHARE?"

Encourage this person to take a task inventory, to outline everything they have their hands on. Then ask, "Do you need to run all of these? Can you reassign some projects, or spend less time on a few?" The same is true with new projects. Suggest a new project moratorium or a limit. The hardest part for this person is letting go. But if you begin by listing the number of low-impact projects they have going, it will become self-evident that they are overextended. And then, if you have the chutzpah, you can ask the most difficult question of all: are they contributing, or just getting in the way? Be careful about when and if you ask.

DELEGATION BENEFITS THE DELEGATOR AND THE DELEGATEE

"If you want it done right, do it yourself" is a terrible myth, and the very antithesis of effective management. If you want to grow, help others to do the same by assigning them more responsibility. People really do learn best by doing it themselves, boosting their confidence by having wins under their belts. Everyone benefits when people delegate well, especially the person clearing his own plate. Remind your control freak that leaders need time to think and strategize, not to mention enjoy life. In truth, the person you're talking to probably already knows the value of what you're saying.

EXPECT "REASONABLE" EXCUSES, AND HAVE REBUTTALS READY

Any good control freak has strong rationales for why they hold all their assignments close to their vests. Your job is to take away their arguments. One standard defense is, "In the time I take to explain it, I can do it myself." Yes, but only once. A single demonstration of how to do something, along with some hands-on guidance, should yield months if not years of others doing the task. Another excuse to expect: "I won't have the answers for my boss when I'm asked." That's a weak comeback because good managers set up reporting systems and communications loops, to make sure they're in the know at all times. There's no reason why the control freak shouldn't be able to answer a question quickly, whether they're personally doing the work or not.

Finally, underlying a great deal of the maniacal need to own all responsibilities is insecurity. One dark possibility—and one few people feel comfortable confessing—is that things may actually turn out well if they cede control. And once they share the assignment with someone else, they'll lose credit for the achievement.

Your job when talking to the control freak is to understand what may live below the surface. And as we said earlier, consider getting outside help if necessary.

4.

Fear—Expect the Worst and Avoid Taking Action

"My mom suggested I narrow down my choice of colleges to eliminate the 'stretch' schools. We have a long list of 'safe' colleges and universities that we're sure will accept me. But my high school guidance counselor thinks I have a shot at some of the upper tier schools, even an Ivy! She thinks we should go for it and apply because she says I have strong enough SATs and grades. But Mom thinks we shouldn't get our hopes up and waste time. She's so afraid that I'll be disappointed, that I think she's holding me back."

Fear is a tough concept to argue with. After all, there are real things to fear. You don't have to be a pessimist to know that relatives get sick; friends lose jobs; companies can behave unethically; people commit crimes in the name of self-interest. Those aren't paranoid thoughts or delusional ramblings. Those are just the facts. Hopes and dreams don't always work out.

In other words, on the balance sheet of life, there's this variable cost called "risk." It's always there, in everything we do. But the degree to which we allow our aversion to risk to hinder our forward motion determines whether we'll take on new challenges and pave new roads; or convince ourselves that the worst is yet to come. And, babe, it won't be fine.

Tish observes, "We know that people with the HeadTrash of fear are self-limiting. They hold themselves back because they see barriers instead of possibilities. But their fear infects others. It's contagious. They create paranoid environments, especially fearful executives and parents. The fallout is that everyone who deals with them becomes frightened. A fearful leader makes people uncomfortable. Everyone else is always covering his or her tracks. People don't take risks. They don't speak up, and they don't offer solutions."

It's easy to picture the scared-stiff company division where an employee's primary mission is to maintain the status quo and stay below the radar. After all, what's the incentive to stick your neck out when your boss is letting you know through his actions that he's not interested in anything more than hanging on to his gig? What he's also doing, however, is holding back the people on his team who are looking to build their careers, too. That leads to a dispirited staff that loses respect for their boss and focuses primarily on protecting themselves.

At home, the byproducts of fear are harder to identify. But fear-influenced parenting can manifest itself by creating a new generation of underachievers. Children who've been sheltered all their lives, kept a little too close to the nest, may resist the chance to go to sleep-away camp with their friends. Or they avoid participating in after-school activities. Inherited parental dread prevents them from auditioning for the school musical. They decide not to go out for the basketball team. They beg off submitting an essay to the school paper. Whatever the dodge, the common theme is avoiding the chance of failing. But what those hesitant parents have forgotten to demonstrate to their children is that they're also avoiding the chance of succeeding.

Fearfulness this extreme expresses a very pessimistic view

of the world. But as the great American philosopher C. S. Peirce (pronounced "purse") argued, pessimism is illogical in the long run, because you can't guarantee that something good won't happen.

Case History: Fear of making "the move" holds a family back

The day after their wedding vows, Jim and Charlotte made a second vow. While categorizing their wedding gifts and getting ready for their honeymoon, they promised each other they would buy a house. "Within a year at most," they said during their pinky swear. They were excited.

But whenever they approached the conversation over the next few months, a new "legitimate" reason popped up, preventing them from taking the next step. Jim wasn't very handy. It was hard to see him maintaining a house. And then there were their careers, which could easily take them to New York City. Why buy a house now when you're only going to sell it a year or two later?

"Within a year at most" had lasted for seven years, when Jim landed the job of his dreams locally. That turn of events triggered the decision to finally buy a house for their growing family, which now included three-year old Kimmy.

Charlotte felt they should skip the conventional starter home and buy a bigger house in a suburb with a good elementary and high school system. They could afford it, plus she knew they wanted to have another child. Now was the time to take the leap! But Jim was reluctant to add more expense to the monthly budget. This was a brand new job; there was no way of knowing how long it would last.

Jim's trepidation trumped Charlotte's vision. They set their sights on a small city row home instead, one whose monthly mortgage payment would equal what they were already paying for rent. "That's fine for now," Charlotte said. "But you know we'll have to move again soon."

Two years later, baby Alexandra arrived, rekindling the conversation about looking for a home in the suburbs. Ah, the suburbs, where they would have a backyard, good schools, their own driveway, and most of all, space! It sounded wonderful—to Charlotte. To Jim, it sounded like more stress. The thought of a higher monthly mortgage on top of adding another person to their health insurance payment, albeit a small and precious person, made his palms sweat. While Alex was a baby, they could get by in the current house, Jim argued. He suggested revisiting the discussion when Kimmy was ready for first grade.

Three years later, while she was packing Kimmy's lunch for the first day of school, Charlotte reminded Jim about their plan to move to the suburbs. "Now is the time, before the girls develop bonds in the neighborhood. And we're running out of room around here," she said.

"Funny you should mention that," Jim replied. "I've been running the numbers and I have a great idea. If we build a room over the garage, we can stay right here! The girls can continue in their schools, and the expense would be half of what we'd pay for a new home in the 'burbs. It keeps our mortgage reasonable and avoids the headache and expense of moving. What do you think?"

What Charlotte thought, as she slowly nodded her head, was that they would never move to the suburbs. Never.

Penny's Perspective: Making it Happen

Fear is debilitating because it delays decision-making, which impedes productivity. One of the characteristics of successful people is their ability to decide quickly and move forward. That's not the same as making a "snap judgment," which is often uninformed. Rather, it is a process of accessing pertinent information and arriving at a conclusion. Fear stops decision-making and can be the root cause of failing to have clarity in business and life. It's easy to attribute fear to a lack of knowledge, because what is ignorance other than a failure to ask questions? In life as on Jeopardy, we need to ASK THE RIGHT QUESTIONS. When you let go of looking for the right answers, and focus instead on finding the right questions, you can overcome that fear and get back on the path to success.

Fear masked with good intentions: Seven signs to look for at home and at work

Fear is a primal response, the fight-or-flight instinct built into our very DNA. It's the reflex that allowed our species to outlast the wooly mammoth. Fear is so powerful, so embedded in us, it triggers physical reactions we can't control. Racing hearts, shaky hands, cold sweats, twitchy eyelids, involuntary nail biting or lip chewing—your charming signals are personal to you. What's universal, however, is that fear can be so overwhelming that it overrides our ability to suppress its physical expression.

While horrible to experience, visible fear is at least pure. We know what's happening because we feel it or see it. Where fear becomes complex is when you or someone you care about is hiding theirs with compensatory behaviors, or denying it even exists. Fear wears many costumes, and can appear practical. Here are seven signs to look for in yourself and the people you want to help.

1. *Procrastination: Put off today what you're afraid of confronting tomorrow*

   As Scarlett O'Hara once said, when confronted with an uncertain future and the steps she should take, "I can't think about that right now. If I do, I'll go crazy. I'll think about that tomorrow. After all, tomorrow is another day."

   Many a decision is delayed due to the terror of taking action—and making the wrong choice. Procrastination is such a popular option because it's so easy to postpone the tough stuff while hoping for a change. And with the pace of life lately, something will certainly come up to distract everyone from what really needs to be done. But serious problems rarely disappear without serious effort, usually requiring choices and changes.

2. *Delegation: Handing off the ugly and avoiding responsibility*

   It's easy to spot the fearful company executive. She's the person who dishes out her dirty work: when one of her staff gets fired, she's not even in the room. At an executive meeting, he brings along a staffer to explain the big project to his bosses.

   The dynamic works the same way in families, too. One parent often plays the heavy, the bouncer responsible for enforcing room cleaning and lawn mowing, the disciplinarian who calls out failing grades or missed curfews. Fear of an uncomfortable conversation, or being disrespected, causes mothers and fathers to abdicate their role as guide and guardian. Which means children learn that boundaries and responsibilities are subjective. Not at all like real life. Many times in business the dynamic is similar, and leaders fear the consequences of having a difficult conversation. Will the employee go into a funk that will hurt performance? Will the person quit? This is the HeadTrash of fear.

3. *Sharing the blame to avoid direct confrontation*
Hang a sign around your neck that reads, "I'm a wuss!" That's the message you send when you call in a group to scold one person. "Everyone else in the room knows what's going on," says Tim. "They know who lost the client, or who's leaving their clothing all over their bedroom floor. But scaredy-cat parents will call a family meeting, or scaredy-cat managers will call a group meeting, to reprimand one person, which only breeds resentment with everyone else in the family or the division."

4. *Diluting the message: Finding the nerve to say less than you should*
Sometimes the conflict-averse person finds the pluck to confront the person in need of a talking to. What they might lose in that moment, however, is the gumption to say what really needs to be said. The words fail them because they've lost the courage to be direct. That results in a verbal dance around the topic, leaving the receiver wondering what their misdeed was, and if there are going to be any consequences at all.

5. *Analysis paralysis*
Endless research is an effective way to avoid making a decision. It looks like you're actually producing something, doing

your homework! This is not to say that we don't need to review the data and generate informed insights to come to a productive solution. But many good decisions were never made because there was always one more piece of information needed. In the world of fear, there's never enough. And while one person is busy triple-checking the answer, another person—usually a competitor—is executing it.

6. *Perfectionism: The search for the unobtainable ideal*
   Pity the perfectionist: he or she will never be happy. What perfectionists seek doesn't exist. They will endlessly miss or extend deadlines in an attempt to produce the perfect product. The goal of many perfectionists, however, is to avoid turning in anything at all. Some won't even start an assignment, or will create a different task, just to avoid failing. Productive high achievers know that the path to greatness begins with "good enough." Getting the work done well enough gets them closer to the finish line, even while they push to make their deliverables even better.

7. *Hypochondria: Imagining illness to petition for a pass*
   Before we walk down this road, a note of caution—people have real illnesses, whether physical or psychological, that may require you or their supervisors to give them some slack. Depending on the situation, employees and family members occasionally need time off or a reduced workload. You can't expect a spouse with a back problem to weed the garden. And sick days exist for a reason. But we all know people who try to lower your demands of them, along with their output, by playing the sick card. For some, it's the only card in the deck. That's a challenging ruse to expose because

it's insensitive and illegal, to deny someone the right to care for themself. And you don't want to intimate that someone is lying, until there is no other choice.

For signs that illness is a proxy for fear, pay attention to when and how frequently that person seeks medical attention. Watch for people who miss meetings they were scheduled to play a role in, or who always have conveniently timed maladies.

Where this becomes especially difficult is with people whose fear becomes psychosomatic, whose stress actually produces headaches, heart palpitations or depression. For people who fall into this category, consider seeking outside counseling and support. Sometimes the best thing you can do for another person is lead them to the ongoing therapy or counseling they need.

AN EXCERPT FROM OUR FIRST HEADTRASH BOOK

Fear versus Caution: Reflexive Flight versus Thoughtful Action

Fear is so hard to overcome because we humans are hardwired for it. Fear, after all, is the survival instinct, the impulse that prompted our ancient ancestors to flee when ugly creatures with big claws and teeth began picturing them as entrées. What could be more sensible than feeling fear when pondering an important personnel change, a major investment, or big presentation? The stakes are high, and fear in these circumstances is just common sense, right? Well, not exactly. Extreme fear often stops executives and managers cold. It's not a speed bump; it's a brick wall. It can render people incapable of taking action because they're too worried about the downsides. So nothing changes. Nothing improves. Nothing gets done.

Compare that with fear's nobler cousin, caution. In its third definition of caution Merriam-Webster describes it as "prudent forethought to minimize risk."

Caution, in other words, recognizes that there really are risks to what we do in business—often large ones. It admits that there are many potential consequences to an action and that not all of them may be good. But caution takes a proactive point of view, considering the whole picture and how to minimize the hazards without losing sight of the upsides.

The expression "proceed with caution" generally captures the best way to handle fear, taking action with an appropriate level of respect for the potential negative outcomes. But before we can learn how to proceed with caution, we need to understand more about the two most common fears in business: fear of making the wrong decision and fear of having a difficult conversation.

Behind the Scenes with Tish & Tim: Fear Anecdote— The consensus builder

Javier considered himself a good boss, the kind of person he would have liked to work for. And now, he was at the highest level he'd ever reached, executive vice president at a Fortune 1000 company. He was really on track. In the new job, Javier's team doubled in size, which of course made life more stressful. That was to be expected. New team members and increased budgets also meant he now had to produce and present even more detailed reports for the scrutiny of senior management.

That also increased the amount of meetings, in a company that was already meeting-crazy. On top of the regular project discussions, and weekly updates with his boss, now Javier was sitting down with the legal and sales teams weekly. Despite those added burdens, the first six months of the new role seemed to be going well. He was hitting his numbers. And he felt that his staff liked and supported him. That's where he was wrong.

The first sign of an insurrection appeared when one of his reports challenged Javier in a meeting in a way that seemed openly hostile. Her style suggested she didn't respect him. Javier knew she spoke that way to other people, but he was her boss! Simple respect was in order. Then another staff member, someone Javier liked personally, began dropping the ball on projects, without explaining in advance why he would be missing deadlines. When Javier confronted him, he seemed to shrug it off.

"From the outside looking in, it was hard to tell what the problem was. Here was a personable guy who seemed to be well liked," Tim said. "Javier had just wrapped up a huge customer service program that was making its mark in the company. It was a mystery that his staff seemed to be turning on him. I thought maybe Javier's assessment was wrong."

In his research, Tim first learned that Javier was having a hard time managing his people.

The next piece of the puzzle Tim put together was that only a few of Javier's projects were making progress. Most of them seemed to be stuck in neutral, if they were even started at all.

What became clear was that Javier had a severe case of fear

HeadTrash. He was putting off moving projects forward because he was terrified that he was going to make wrong decisions. Further, he was having a very difficult time holding his direct reports accountable, unable or unwilling to have the difficult conversations with them about poor performance.

Soon, the team smelled Javier's fear. And even though they liked him as a person, they came to feel that he could not lead the team effectively. Ironically, Javier pictured himself as a consensus builder, but the truth was he couldn't get past his own fear and his team was frustrated that he couldn't make a decision.

It didn't take long for Javier's boss to realize what was happening. Eventually, Javier lost control of his team and his boss starting making the decisions Javier was unable or unwilling to make. Javier's fear HeadTrash cost him his job.

Caution versus fear: Pausing versus stopping dead

It's two o'clock in the morning. You're driving home from a party when you roll up to an intersection with a blinking red light, the kind that allows you to proceed as long as no cars are coming in either direction. Think of fear as the mental state that would keep you stuck at the light all night, anticipating a car that might show up out of nowhere, while you're waiting for a green light. The green light to go is a traffic signal the person with fear Head-Trash can't see.

Caution, conversely would have you stop, look both ways to make sure you can proceed safely, and then go. It's the courage to proceed sensibly.

"We are not advocating being reckless," Tish says. "I'm a risk taker; that's how I built my business. But I'm not rash. We are not suggesting that people take on subprime mortgages or leap into situations without doing their research." In other words, don't let fear shut you down before you begin. Act! But use your judgment.

Merriam-Webster defines caution as "prudent forethought to minimize risk."

Prudent forethought is another way of saying perform all your research. Look at the possibilities, and the dangers. Go ahead and assemble your data and insights. But then do something. Proceed with caution, but do proceed. A cautious person who has done her homework develops courage.

A Fear Checklist and Comparison

HOW TO IDENTIFY FEAR HEADTRASH IN SOMEONE YOU KNOW.

FEARFUL PEOPLE . . .	COURAGEOUS PEOPLE . . .
Avoid confronting poor performance or neglected tasks by ignoring them, stalling, or offering "workarounds"	Will have difficult conversations with employees, family and friends about what needs to change and why
Are reluctant to try new things because of the potential negative outcomes of change	Despite resistance, embrace new ideas and drive change by setting clear expectations
Will not stand up for something they strongly believe in if it's not fully accepted by others	Have the courage of their convictions and will attempt to influence others who might not be in agreement yet
Hire individuals like themselves whom they feel they can control	Surround themselves with a diverse team of varied views and talents
Can become paralyzed in the face of a difficult decision for fear of making a mistake	Recognize that failure sometimes happens, but that decisiveness is critical to success

(continued)

FEARFUL PEOPLE . . .	COURAGEOUS PEOPLE . . .
Will not admit when he doesn't know something for fear it will make him look weak and incapable	Is comfortable disclosing he doesn't know everything, and relies on the knowledge, skills and experience of others to solve problems and advance

HeadTrash Alert! A Quick Quiz on Fear

TO ASSESS WHETHER SOMEONE YOU KNOW HAS FEAR HEADTRASH, USE THE FOLLOWING QUIZ:

	Never	Sometimes	Often	Always
1. Is afraid to have difficult conversations.				
2. Repeatedly imagines worst-case outcomes for any decision.				
3. Obsesses over the same issues repeatedly.				
4. Under the guise of "needing more data," delays decisions.				
5. Will settle for the status quo, even if it affects progress.				
6. Accepts questionable behaviors from employees who are critical to the business or close family members.				
7. Struggles with carrying out decisions that others might think are harsh.				

If you checked "often" or "always" three or more times, the person in question probably has fear HeadTrash.

What I (Tish) do to help my clients begin to overcome fear is to ask them, "How will you feel if you don't take the risk. What are you sacrificing?" People need to ask the hard question, what are they giving up by not taking the risk? If they reflect on it for a while, it can be profound, and can be a trigger for change.

(Tim) That is a powerful question. What you're asking is, what does regret look like? People who are fearful only picture failure or rejection. It helps to have someone say, "What if you didn't do it? What are you giving up?" From there we can create a positive scenario, and portray what is possible.

How do fearful people function in a world they just *know* is dangerous?

To introduce his movie masterpiece *The Twelve Chairs*, Mel Brooks shows the opening credits over the song "Hope for the best. Expect the worst." Hope? For people who are fearful, the second verse is the only verse. But it's more complicated than morbid pessimism. Challenges are threats, questions are accusations, and obstacles are to be avoided at all costs.

"Fear is concern with what is happening outside of us," says Tim. "It's profound worry over external events and the inability to accept being wrong. People with severe fear want an out."

The "out" is finding ways to dodge responsibility, decisions, and actions. Fear-based people will do anything to avoid exposing themselves to failure or embarrassment, including doing the very things that guarantee failing. Here are some tools you can provide them with to help them reduce the fright, which makes room for courage to grow.

PRACTICE. MAKE THE SMALL DECISIONS; THE BIGGER ONES WILL FOLLOW

People in fear inertia have forgotten how to make and act on decisions, which is not surprising since they've put so much energy into avoiding them. One of the best things you can do for people with fear is to show them how to make smaller decisions first, and then increase the stakes. Give them some practice with making choices and carrying them out. And remind them that whether they know it or not, they're making decisions every day. What's for dinner? What should I wear to school? When should I leave the house for work? Decisions every one. Develop a process that lets them up the ante.

FEEL THE FEAR. IT'S OKAY AND NORMAL

Author Susan Jeffers said it best in the title of her classic book: *Feel the Fear and Do it Anyway*. In the introduction, she tips her hat to fear, acknowledging that when we attempt new things, we may feel ill at ease. And that's just fine. "Whenever we take a chance and enter unfamiliar territory or put ourselves into the world in a new way, we experience fear. Very often this fear keeps us from moving ahead with our lives," she writes. "The trick is to feel the fear and do it anyway." In other words, don't try to fool yourself or someone you're working with that they're not feeling fear. It's real, and you feel it. So go ahead and feel it. But also, go ahead!

MISTAKES WILL HAPPEN. LEAVE ROOM FOR ERRORS IN ADVANCE

Along with death and taxes, here's another thing you can be certain of. You will make mistakes. We all do. No matter how prepared or resolved you are, expect to make a wrong decision, or to handle a situation poorly. If you or the person you're coaching accepts this going in, everyone will be more likely to press forward despite the setbacks. That's called learning as you go. When the people around know that you're evaluating all the information and forging ahead confidently, they'll come along, even if you have been proven wrong. The key is to admit mistakes, act decisively to fix the error, and then move on.

Even better, imagine the worst-case scenarios in advance and decide what you will do if they happen. Put another way, prepare Plan B. Having a backup strategy can offer precious peace of mind. That will allow you to be ready with an alternate action plan should the best-laid plan not work out.

IF YOU'RE GOING TO MAKE UP A STORY, MAKE IT POSITIVE

What is fear when you strip everything else away? It's our negative self-talk, the noise in our own heads, the worst-case scenarios we imagine that turn fiction into friction.

But we can also use our imaginations to picture positive outcomes. What if things work out? What if a decision takes your family or business someplace positive? What would that look like? Having people picture the positive, also called "visualization," can produce dramatic results. Athletes and performers swear by it. Imagining success versus failure can actually alter thinking and emotions. It produces positive feelings, and can be a step toward developing confidence.

SEEK OUTSIDE ASSISTANCE WHEN NECESSARY

To work through their fears about specific decisions, or to take on an intractable personal roadblock, the person you want to help may need to consult a third party. As we said throughout this book, some problems are beyond our unaided abilities. Don't hesitate to seek support from an outside expert, therapist, spiritual advisor, counselor, or a psychologist.

THE 2-PART REALITY CHECK: 1. LIFE ISN'T ALWAYS FAIR; 2. HOW BAD IS IT REALLY?

A service you can offer a fearful person is the 2-Part Reality Check.

1. *Part 1. Life isn't always fair.*
   Yes, many companies will work your tail off and overlook your major contributions. And sure, your parents may have screwed up your childhood and denied you support that others had growing up. The list of justifications for fear is long. But that's life, and it's often unkind. With few exceptions, it doesn't excuse anyone from attempting to move forward. How else can we improve our realities? We do better when we accept the facts, and begin working with them.

2. *Part 2. Is it as bad as we think?*
   Part of your task as the person helping another overcome their fear may be to ask, "Is it as bad as you think?" When you catch people "catastrophizing," call it out. Disrupt their entrenched "life is harsh" philosophy.

TO LESSEN THE RISK, TAKE IT IN DOSES

One of the reasons fearful people have trouble tackling big tasks is that they think they have to climb the whole mountain in a day. "We don't have to take on the whole kahuna at once. We tell people that one of the ways to overcome fear is to take things in small steps. Break it down," Tish says. You can lessen risk by doing things in stages, committing to pieces of the assignment, a step at a time.

GIVE YOURSELF A SAFETY NET

A few years ago, the son of one of Tish's colleagues had just been accepted into New York University's law school. As he was already renting an apartment in the city, the easy thing to do would have been to have him stay put and absorb the annual rent increases. Another option would have been to help him move to yet another NYC apartment, his fourth in five years. But his father, regretful that he hadn't bought a building for his own businesses over the years, chafed at the thought of three added years of escalating New York rents. He volunteered a crazy suggestion: "Let's buy a condominium," he said to the family. At $450,000 to $500,000 minimum for a 700-square foot apartment in Brooklyn, Tish's colleague thought her husband had lost his mind. But he countered, "For the three years that he's in law school, we have a tenant; even longer if he gets a job in New York." In other words, they had a safety net. So they bought the condo. "There were months where it was tough meeting the bills, and we wondered what we had done. There was some scrimping and scraping, for sure," said Tish's colleague. But now, five years later, the practicing lawyer still lives in the apartment, and is very happy there. And as a bonus, said Tish's colleague, "The value of the condo has risen dramatically. Our son has a great place to live, and we'll turn a profit. It was a great decision."

FIND YOUR VOICE

One simple way to begin neutralizing the fear we hear in our heads is to add our voice to conversations. What do you think, what do you stand for? Speak up! Have a say! By putting yourself into discussions at home and at work, you start combating fear with your words. You establish your presence, which can create a runway for braver actions.

POSITIVE REINFORCEMENT: CATCH SOMEONE DOING SOMETHING RIGHT

For a fearful person, positive reinforcement is powerful medicine. It's an ongoing antidote to all the negative self-talk they've been telling themselves. What may seem like a cliché, or a small obvious courtesy, can be the spark that starts the fire. Calling out a success publicly, or taking people aside and letting them know that they handled a situation well, builds confidence. And that's one thing a fearful person really needs. When you accentuate the positive you rewrite someone else's script. Sincere praise, delivered at the right time by the right person, can be the building block on which someone fashions a positive future.

REGRET IN ADVANCE: HOW DO YOU FEEL ABOUT MISSING SUCCESS?

One of the most powerful exercises in this book, the one exercise everyone should perform wherever they are in their lives, is to *regret in advance*. Instead of thinking about how hard it will be to take action, or what happens if you fail, ponder what you're giving up by NOT taking action. What are you missing if you don't proceed with your goal? "It helps to have someone raise the question of 'What if you didn't do it? How will you feel? What will you regret?' Sometimes you have to ask the question out loud," says Tish.

Regretting in advance lets us envision a future we didn't create due to inaction. Prospective remorse can then prompt us to move ahead and create a better future.

Penny's Perspective

What are the odds? How to avoid thinking yourself into fear

Here's a great tool to help fearful people stop the doubt train before it gets on the tracks. Before you worry yourself into a fear state, ask the following three questions:

1. *What is the likelihood this will actually occur?*
2. *What would have to happen for it to occur?*
3. *What could you do to prevent this from occurring?*

Your answers will create a risk-management situation for calculating the possibilities and planning ahead, thus removing fear. Being prepared has a way of making us more productive and eliminating or drastically reducing negative emotions.

5

Guilt—Two Sides of a Very Expensive Coin

"No matter how much I did for him, I always felt like I was letting him down. Whether I took time off from work repeatedly to run his errands, or if I rescheduled something I had planned with the kids, it just didn't matter. His needs were always more important than mine. He never actually said that, but he always found a way to convey it. He knew how to push my buttons to get what he wanted. And if I didn't give in, I was just a bad daughter."

Guilt can have a profoundly negative impact on both work and personal life. When the guilt-wielding relative or employee is on their game, they can get just about anything they want, whenever they want it. Superb guilt-wielders know whether to pour it on with a ladle, or to dress it up with desperation or urgency. And one of the reasons that guilt can be so effective is that it truly is a double-edged sword.

There are people who are skilled at serving it up, and others who seem genetically predisposed to responding to it. Put a guilt-wielder together with a guilt-ridden person and in almost every exchange you have a winner and a loser.

Now, compared to, say, control or arrogance or fear, guilt may seem like a fluffy HeadTrash, a softball eccentricity in a world of hardball dysfunction. Nothing could be further from the truth. Guilt is a lever that moves mountains. In part that is because feeling guilt is normal.

If you've actually done something you know is wrong, or are about to engage in a self-absorbed act that may wound someone else, you'll probably feel badly. That pang of conscience, that angel on your shoulder, is what separates healthy humans from psychopaths. If you didn't feel it sometimes we'd be worried about you. But if you or someone you care about often feels guilt without a valid reason, if you're being "guilted" into doing things you don't want to do, this chapter is for you. Likewise, if you know someone who uses guilt repeatedly and unethically to achieve their own agenda, read on.

Just how powerful is guilt? Tish observes that "grown adults will pursue jobs they never wanted because their parents have made it clear they'd be disappointed if they did anything else." To second the point, Tim offers another common example. "Children will attend colleges that weren't even on their short lists. We're talking about whole lives being redirected and spent doing things you dislike just so you won't let your family down. That's power."

And don't discount the effects of guilt at the office. Look around the halls for a long-time team member who doesn't pull his weight or a staffer who's bounced from one role to another, boomeranging around the building in search of a skill set. Somewhere above each no-talent staff member is probably a guilt-ridden executive who can't bring himself to end the game of musical chairs and let someone go.

Don't let guilt push you around

Guilt can goad you into keeping employees who are not benefiting the team, or prevent you from taking action to hire the right person. Hiring the daughter of a friend who once performed the Heimlich maneuver on you may make you feel like you repaid a debt. But if you have to "carry" this person for years to come, you're discrediting your whole team—unless, of course, this person would have been a first candidate to start with.

Case History: Career path takes a guilt trip

When they first moved in together, and through the early years of their marriage, Hillary and Alan followed their strategy to the letter. Both of them would work, but he would be the breadwinner. His career would take precedence, providing the sustaining income and foundation on which they would build their future. Hers would serve as a secondary salary, financing their savings and contributing to their fund for special occasions. That was the plan.

But a funny thing happened on the way to the office. As the years progressed, so did she, getting recognized and pulled up the corporate ladder as one boss after the other applauded her technology and management skills. She grew with the company, rising from assistant to divisional manager. And while she was going up, he was going sideways, hitting a wall at the manager level, and never breaking through to the next rung. He made jokes about her someday passing him, jibes that were supposed to be funny but seemed intended to make her feel bad as well. "Geez, Hon," he said, laughing. "If this keeps up, *you'll be the breadwinner.*"

It struck a sour chord with her, even if that wasn't his intention—almost as if he wanted her to feel guilty for succeeding. But because they were on the same level, she attributed the knot in her stomach to misinterpreting his sense of humor.

When she got the call from HR, it was a surprise. Someone in senior management was a secret admirer of her work and had suggested her for a director's role in his division. The HR person said she would have to apply and interview for the job along with the other candidates. But he made clear during their conversation that because she was a known performer, she would have an inside track if everything else was in order.

If she applied for the job and got it, there would be more responsibility, significantly more money and benefits, and opportunity for even more advancement.

She was excited. She was terrified. She was conflicted.

That night over dinner, she replayed the HR conversation for her husband, sharing her enthusiasm while making it clear that she valued his input. She described the job, her impressions of the future boss, where this could take her in the company. She made it clear that this role would be more time consuming. Then she said she wanted to go for it, but she wouldn't do it without his support. She stopped talking and waited to hear his reaction, holding her breath.

After a long pause, he managed a weak smile and said, "I'm really happy for you. Congratulations. My concern is that we're not following the plan."

"What are you talking about?" she said.

"Well, we agreed from the beginning that I would be the lead income, and that we'd focus on my career. I feel like this changes everything, even though I know this is a big opportunity. I just wonder if this is the right thing," he said. "What do you think?"

Her heart sank. This was the best thing that had ever happened in her career, the kind of opportunity that could lead to the corporate suite. So why did she feel bad about it? Why was her husband, who was supposed to be her cheerleader, looking so glum and hapless? Her head was spinning. She didn't know whether to cry or scream.

"I need to get some air," she said, and headed for the front door.

"What's wrong?" her husband said.

"I don't know. I have to think about this and I can't do it here. Not in this room with you." She grabbed her coat, car keys, and purse, and left without saying goodbye.

She got into her car and started driving, not knowing where she was going or why. The seatbelt felt like it was choking her, so she pulled over to undo it. When she came to a stop, she burst into tears, and then started pounding the dashboard, screaming and punching the padding. Then suddenly, like a storm that had ended, she became calm. Her cell phone rang. She recognized her home phone number.

"Hi. Are you okay?" said her husband, in an imploring tone that was asking multiple questions in one sentence.

"I wasn't," she said. "I was awful. But I'm better now."

"Good," he said.

"Yep, I have clarity," she said. "I'm taking that job, and you are going to support my decision, because what's good for me is good for you, too. It damn well better be."

Guilty! Of being guilt-wielding or guilt-ridden: Seven signs to look for at home and at work

Guilt is a sucker's game, a con the wielder runs on the guilt-ridden. The guilt-ridden person often doesn't even know he or she is responding to a ploy, particularly when the game is among family. And no good deed will go unpunished, because once you fall for a guilt-wielder's machinations, you're their mark forever, unless, that is, you can identify their scams and learn to set boundaries. Here are some of the frauds you or someone you care about may be falling for or perpetrating.

1. *Guilt-wielding 1: Feel sorry for me*
    You never want to deny support to a person truly in need. But some friends and family members seem to always be in need—constantly sick, or short of cash, or depressed and stressed. They use their bad fortune to good effect, making their problems yours even when they seem quite able to help themselves. Sure, your brother can drive himself to the doctor. He has a car. But he reminds you that he hates to go alone, even for a routine physical, "because it makes my blood pressure go up, and they get a false reading." And you wouldn't want that to happen, would you?

2. *Guilt-wielding 2: The over reactor. The future of the world is at stake!*
    The stakes are always high for the guilt-slinging over reactor. She (or he) attempts to manage your emotions by portraying all the harm you may do by not complying with her plans. Do you really want your daughter to feel inadequate at her own prom? What price self-esteem, Dad? Actually, $650 for

her prom gown and another $150 for the shoes. A life of feeling unworthy and unloved can be avoided, and years of therapy averted simply by breaking out the credit card. In short, watch out for people who dramatically inflate the potential problems to achieve a self-interested solution.

3. *Guilt-wielding 3: I speak for a higher authority*
Uncle Jack has been dead for 15 years. Fortunately, Aunt Mary is still alive and is apparently something of a psychic. She speaks for him in the hereafter, interpreting exactly how Uncle Jack would like you to behave! Beware the person who invokes the names of deceased relatives and friends in order to maneuver you into their way of thinking. These guilt trippers call upon higher authorities to endow them with the right to tell you what to do. And they don't only rob graves:

- They also appropriate religion: "The Bible says. . . ."

- They cite tradition: "But you have to come. The family has always gotten together on Sundays."

- They co-opt the moral high ground: "You know it's the right thing to do."

By not caving in to their demands, you not only disappoint them, but also disobey some greater mystical forces at work, which can make a person feel very guilty.

1. *Guilt-ridden 1: The self-effacer*
Let's be honest. Some people are just gifted, hitting the born-this-good lottery in one way or another. They're exceptionally

talented. They're smarter than the average bear. They're uncommonly comely. That's life! If you are among the fortunate few holding one of those tickets, be happy! Capitalize on your good fortune and get on with your success. Why be shy about it?

Sadly, those who are guilt-ridden could give you many reasons to be shy about it, among them a sense of unworthiness for the gifts fate bestowed on them or a discomfort about what's expected of people to whom great opportunity was given. At the root of both is guilt about perhaps having it easier than their fellow man or woman. They wear their potential like sackcloth, apologizing with guilt for the natural competence that the rest of us have to earn through grit.

2. *Guilt-ridden 2: Stuck in neutral. Unable to do what needs to be done*

There are times at home and at work when a leader has to stand up and demand that someone do better. Holding people accountable requires chutzpah, and can make some bosses and parents feel uncomfortable. Even more challenging is when accountability fails and a child should be disciplined, or an employee dismissed. Reprimands delayed metastasize over time, morphing from discomfort to ongoing guilt and avoidance. Look, Andi really is busy at school, and taking away her iPhone because her clothing is always all over the floor feels so severe. And Charlie may be a terrible employee, but he has a family to feed. If we put some people around him, he's really not as bad as he appears.

So what happens?

At home, mom starts picking up the clothes in time for the laundry. At the office, a work-around is agreed upon, placing

the failing employee in a new role, as HR plays the ever popular game, Musical Headcount.

3. *Guilt-ridden 3: Numb from too much arm twisting*
   The guilt dance typically requires two to tango. A wielder
   usually needs a feeler to do his bidding; otherwise the goading and psychological arm-twisting falls on deaf ears. In the
   beginning, the partners move in lockstep, the wielder hitting all the right emotional buttons, the feeler carrying out
   the tasks reflexively—martinet and marionette each playing
   their roles. But eventually, a feeler can go numb, her emotional receptors dulled, her radar on alert after having her
   strings pulled one too many times. And what was once that
   employee's sincere response to a boss's request becomes little
   more than a compliance action. The feeler wants only to do
   the minimum because she knows she's being used. She no
   longer trusts the motivations of the wielder.

4. *Guilt-ridden 4: Giving away the prizes you've earned to
   be "fair"*
   Face it. Life is competitive. It's not always fair or predictable,
   but one thing we know for sure is that there are winners and
   losers. And sometimes, based on their performance, the
   winners truly are deserving of the promotions or the plumb
   assignments. Good things do often come to those who've
   earned them. But like the Self-Effacers who can't enjoy the
   talents they were born with, the Givers hand off the hon-
   ors they've worked for, sharing the spoils because they feel
   a sense of shame around their recognition. They're misinterpreting the parable "It's better to give than receive." To maintain a false sense of security, Givers will share assignments or

assign kudos to the unworthy. While it's always good to credit the team after a win, it's bad to distribute props to someone undeserving. The message is that no one really is exceptional, and that everyone gets a gold star just for showing up.

Behind the Scenes with Tish & Tim: Guilt Anecdote—The too-good son and the opportunist mother

In family situations, guilt is an especially potent weapon. You can't see it; you can't touch it. But like an electromagnetic energy, you absolutely know when it's in the room with you. Tim had a client whose mother was a first-rate guilt-wielder. "According to my client, his mom had special powers. She was a like sci-fi character, able to harness and direct guilt at will to coax people to do her bidding," Tim said.

As the good son who was eager to do right by a woman who had lost her husband a few years earlier, Phil was particularly susceptible to her manipulations. To help her through the grieving, and relocate her where he could look after her, he encouraged his mom to sell her house and move near him.

He soon learned that a few blocks away was not close enough. Mom actually wanted to live in his house, and would remind him overtly or covertly every waking minute. "Phil was accustomed to his mother's behavior, but his wife came to detest the conniving. It was another layer of resentment on top of her unannounced visits and expectation to be invited for dinner every night," said Tim.

After all, Phil was already very involved in his mother's life. Recently laid off, Phil—at his mother's urging—drove her to medical appointments. He also went grocery shopping with her, and dropped her at the hairdresser. Even though mom was quite capable of driving herself, Phil played the good son/chauffeur, as he continued looking for a job. "You know I don't like to be alone," was one of the phrases she used to keep Phil behind the wheel.

While he was waiting for his mother in her doctor's office, his cell phone rang. He recognized the number and stepped outside to talk to the vice president of HR at a company that seemed very interested in him. After three rounds of interviews, they had decided to make him an offer, and a very attractive one at that! He was walking on air. His mother came out of the doctor's office, and after she scheduled her next appointment, Phil said, "Mom, I have great news. You know that job I was interviewing for. I got it! They made me an offer!"

Her face went white, a frost overtaking her eyes. He thought he heard her curse under her breath. Then she looked up and said, "Well, make sure you mark down my next appointment. You'll want to tell your new boss that you have to drive your mother to the doctor's office because you don't like her going alone."

"It's hard to believe that a mother is unable to feel immediate joy for her son in the moment," says Tim. "But many people who play the guilt card are narcissistic and/or passive-aggressive. They're used to getting what they want, often because the people around them don't establish boundaries between acceptable and unacceptable behavior. This woman's son, for example, never drew any boundaries. He didn't know how."

Through a series of coaching sessions, we helped Phil become more aware of his feelings of guilt and how he was being manipulated. We also taught him how to respond to his mother's guilt more rationally and take a problem solving approach to her needs as opposed to merely reacting. For instance, Phil hired a driver to take his mother to her various appointments, despite her protestations. In this way, Phil was able to fulfill his obligations to his mom while still living his own life.

Stop guilt-wielding: Replace manipulation with inspiration

No doubt about it. Guilt can get the job done. Leveraging someone's sense of appreciation toward you for a past favor, or squeezing his or her heart with your family bond can generate the right result—the first few times around.

But after that, the person you've been emotionally extorting either wises up and tells you to pound sand, or cooperates resentfully. And their resentment diminishes the quality and timeliness of the work done on your behalf.

The reason is that guilt is an external feeling, forced upon another person through emotional manipulations. And no one likes having their strings pulled, especially when they realize it after the fact. So guilt, powerful though it may be, can evoke an adverse reaction from the person who isn't buying in.

On the flip side is *Inspiration,* emphasis on the syllable, "In." Inspiration is the opposite of guilt and manipulation *because it comes from inside the person you're hoping to influence.* Something you said or did triggers a positive response and generates the desire in someone else to perform at a higher level. An effective method of positive motivation is the classic W-I-F-M: What's In It For Me? How will the person who is doing the task benefit? What will they gain by accomplishing your mission? Money? Career growth? Glory? Self-satisfaction? Less clutter? Less worry? There are so many ways to inspire someone because there are so many rewards.

So if inspiration can be effective, what stops people from using it instead of guilt?

"For many executives and parents, guilt and control are the default settings. 'Just do it because I said so,' or 'I'm your boss,' or 'You don't want to disappoint your husband,'" says Tish. "We've all done that, and it obviously works. But it's also a reflex. The harder thing to do is to spend time understanding what makes the other person tick, and then articulating your needs from their perspective. That takes time and extra effort. But it's worth it. That's what effective leaders do."

Beyond guilt: Compassion instead of obligation

The opposite of guilt is clinical efficiency, acting on whatever needs to be done with a complete lack of sentiment. Someone has to be fired? Your daughter needs to be disciplined? A romantic interest is due for a talking to? Take it on and move on. Do what needs to be done, minus the emotion. This is a nice concept in theory, but not always easy for guilt-ridden people, who often think with their hearts.

The near and healthier cousin to guilt is compassion. Merriam-Webster defines compassion as a "sympathetic consciousness of others' distress together with a desire to alleviate it."

Acting with conscious compassion means that you're aware of your feelings, and that you're the manager of your responses instead of being an unconscious puppet. You can decide to be caring but firm, because you choose to. Or you can decide to bring the hammer down, because you choose to. In short, it's a choice, *your choice*, not a reflex, that drives your actions. And everyone is better for it. Especially you.

A Guilt Checklist and Comparison

HOW TO IDENTIFY GUILT HEADTRASH IN SOMEONE YOU KNOW.

GUILT-INFLICTING PEOPLE . . .	GUILT-RIDDEN PEOPLE . . .	COMPASSIONATE/ INSPIRING PEOPLE . . .
Capitalize on others' weaknesses and pushing emotional buttons	Create "workarounds" or reassign people instead of having difficult conversations	Make an honest and compelling case for what really needs to be done
Seek, get, and are content with simple adherence	Will do anything to avoid conflict	Inspire commitment among engaged relatives and employees
Prey on emotions	Are ruled by emotions	Are willing to have difficult conversations, and do "the right thing"
Use the past to coax others into doing what they want	Avoid the tough stuff, which delays business and personal growth and success	Employ communication and empathy to take the best actions for all
Create lose/lose situations by forcing competent people to protect favored family members or employees	"Protect" people to avoid uncomfortable situations	Act decisively about promotions, demotions, dismissals, or disappointments
Cause frustration and failure by putting poor performers in other departments	Play musical chairs with people in Band-Aid solutions that don't solve performance problems	Refuse to move people into roles for which they are unsuited or unproven

HeadTrash Alert! A Quick Quiz on Guilt

TO ASSESS WHETHER SOMEONE YOU KNOW HAS GUILT HEADTRASH, USE THE FOLLOWING QUIZ:

	Never	Sometimes	Often	Always
1. Often uses "parental guilt" to manipulate family members and business associates to do something.				
2. Holds back from making leadership decisions at work or at home because of personal relationships.				
3. Rationalizes bad behaviors (like embarrassing someone publicly) by feeling badly long enough to make it ok.				
4. Uses guilt to manipulate others to get things done.				
5. Has "guilted" people into doing things so often that it has become a default tactic.				
6. Creates obstacles to moving forward by re-living past experiences that evoke guilt.				

If you checked "often" or "always" three or more times, the person in question probably has guilt HeadTrash.

(Tish) Feeling guilt prevents people from addressing the real issues. You have to stop getting emotional. You have to separate your emotion from what you have to do. Ask what has to change in the office or at home to achieve the goal. Until you get the emotion out of it, and stop skating around it, you'll never make progress.

I (Tim) agree. We have to confront guilt head on. To do that, we have to tell the truth. People who are putting up with bosses or relatives have guilt, and are not making good choices. I'm wondering how many employees would feel comfortable talking openly about guilt with a boss or even a friend. Guilt gets in the way of tough choices. But that's where the growth is.

Advising people with guilt-ridden or guilt-wielding HeadTrashes

As with all HeadTrashes, the person offering the coaching will need to be patient and persistent. Personal growth takes time. But working with guilt is particularly tricky, because the person who's trying to initiate change with a guilt-ridden or guilt-wielding person is confronting two sets of ingrained behaviors.

If you've read this far, you know that for every guilt-wielder there is usually a guilt-ridden person, waiting to hear the music to dance to. And vice versa. You, Mr. or Ms. Change Maker, may actually be rocking a few boats while trying to steer one. Here are some tips and tools to share that can help break the cycle. As we said in other chapters, however, if the task seems too large for you or the person you're trying to help, don't hesitate to seek outside help.

GUILT-RIDDEN TIP 1: SEE THE CLUES

People who respond to the scheming petitions of others have been doing it for so long, they often don't even recognize the ploys that pull their chains. They just react, shutting down their critical brain and never bothering to wonder, "What's happening here?" But there are clues that you can share with a guilt-ridden person to let them know they've been manipulated.

- Are you doing something you really don't want to do?
  - "Are you acting out of a sense of obligation versus free will? That's a sure sign," Tim says. "If it feels bad, your internal BS meter is talking to you."

- Are you afraid of the consequences if you refuse the request?
  - Are you worried about getting a raft of garbage from your mother in-law for not attending the family picnic? Afraid that if you don't watch football with the guys that you'll disappoint your spouse and create a rift? If you feel the pain of a negative payback even as the question is being asked, you're in the guilt zone.

- Is the person asking being authentic?
  - In other words, is this person making an honest direct request, or trying to sneak in the backdoor of "you owe me?" The character of the person doing the asking often tells you everything you need to know.

GUILT-RIDDEN TIP 2: LEARN TO SAY NO

"No" is one of the most powerful words in the English language, particularly in guilt-driven relationships. It sets a boundary for the person who is otherwise accustomed to using guilt, while empowering the guilt-ridden person, who often feels helpless when "guilted" into doing something. The guilt-wielder learns that this other person can defend himself or herself. And the guilt-ridden person sees that it is possible to escape from the cage of unfair obligation.

Tim says, "At some point you have to get out of what I call debtors' prison. You can't allow appreciation for a favor done a decade ago, or gratitude to your family for their support, to rule the rest of your life. The get-out-of-jail card, the key that turns the lock, is the word 'no.'"

But how do you actually say no? For a person accustomed to saying yes, some lessons might be in order. As an exercise, ask yourself how you would you say no to a salesperson trying to persuade you to spend more money than you had in mind. You would be direct, definitive, and composed. You'd probably explain, in no uncertain terms, why you can't oblige them. And you'd do it unemotionally, mainly because you wouldn't feel like you owed the salesperson anything beyond a simple explanation.

And there you have it. The goal is to offer a clear, fear-free rebuke, without raising your voice. Your even tone will let the other person know that you've thought it over, and that you're no longer susceptible to their manipulations. Your calm demeanor might also calm the other person, even as they're getting the bad news. By the way, this will take practice, which may mean writing down what you want to say and rehearsing a few times until it feels natural.

GUILT-RIDDEN TIP 3: CATCH A GUILT-WIELDER IN THE ACT

Svengalis who've gotten their way for years, guilt-wielders grow comfortable employing their dark magic. It's automatic. They push the emotional button, say the daunting phrase, turn the screw just so, and PRESTO! You're suddenly doing exactly what they want. Unless, of course, the person on the other end calls them on it.

"The guilt-ridden person is not addressing what is actually happening. And if he doesn't, he just wallows in his own misery," says Tish. "One of the only ways to address this behavior is to point it out while it's happening. You have to let the other person know that you recognize what is going on and that the jig is up!"

But as with most uncomfortable messages, it's easier thought than said out loud to the person who needs to hear it. Highlighting the problem can be the psychological equivalent of trying to stop a hurricane. Expect denials and rationalizations, resistance and recriminations. Also, don't count on undoing years of behavior in one conversation. Shining a spotlight on the truth, however, is a powerful way to demonstrate that the old regime is about to change, and that you have a say in what's to come.

GUILT-RIDDEN TIP 4: LEARN TO DRAW BOUNDARIES

Who's responsible for making you do things you really don't want to do, for messing with your mind until you get in line? You, actually. The person who feels the guilt is responsible.

"If you're on the receiving end of guilt, you have to learn to draw emotional boundaries," says Tim. "Sometimes even physical boundaries. You have to learn to say no, and the first person you have to correct is yourself."

It's much easier for a guilt-ridden person to wish their boss didn't push their buttons, or their wife was more reasonable.

But if you're coaching that person, you have to help him or her understand that it's *their* responsibility to draw a line in the sand and let the wielder know, the guilt stops here. That starts with the guilt-ridden person's recognizing that he or she is entitled to their own feelings, opinions, and values. Self-worth sets the stage for self-determination, which is a fancy way of saying, "I'll decide whether I want to do this or not, whether I want to feel this way or not."

The gift you can give your friends, staffers, and family members is to remind them that it's their life. And the more time they spend giving it away because they fear the resentment of another person, the more they'll regret it when they finally find the resolve to do what's truly in their own best interests.

GUILT-WIELDER TIP 1: ASK YOURSELF, "CAN IT WAIT?"

Why do guilt-wielders say hurtful, spiteful things? Why do they go right to the jugular? Because they want to make something happen now, and they know how to rattle your cage. "The unfortunate thing is that while they're getting immediate satisfaction, they're also creating long-term disengagement," says Tish. "What guilt-wielders must learn to do is stop themselves from taking advantage of others. They need to ask themselves, 'Do I really need that from this person right now? Is it so important that I need to remind the person that I got him his job 10 years ago and he owes me?'"

If you're a guilt-wielder, this will be challenging, because as we said earlier, wielders throw the guilt switch instinctively. It's what you do because it's what you've always done. And now, we're asking you to remove a big lever from your tool kit.

GUILT-WIELDER TIP 2: ASK WHAT'S BEST FOR THE OTHER PERSON

Talk about turning the tables on yourself. Good guilt-wielders may understand how to move people into action with psychological ploys, but they rarely wonder what it's like to walk in that person's shoes. So instead of going directly into gimme-this mode, pause for a minute and ask yourself a couple of questions. What does this person need? Will this action be in his or her best interests, too? That may sound counterproductive. But the question may prompt a more authentic path to get your needs met, too. Looking for a way to solve your problem and fulfill other people is the win/win we're all looking for.

6

Insecurity—When Self-Doubt Wins Out

> "Having him as a manager is getting frustrating. I genuinely like him as a person, and I think he's really smart. He's also fun to work with. But he can't make a decision to save his life, so nothing moves forward. We'll never hit our numbers that way."

Postponed presentations. Delayed decisions. Missed deadlines. The manager this person is describing is a world-class procrastinator, putting off until tomorrow what should have been done yesterday. With the undependable dawdler, it's easy to think that the issue is time management, writing off his foot dragging as a project administration problem.

But if you look a little deeper, and think about the common thread running through his every unproductive behavior, you might see that insecurity is at its core. After all, what would you do if your first and last thought was that every major presentation would reveal your ineptitude? Most likely, you'd look for compensating actions, psychological workarounds that would save you from being put in situations where you just know that you'll fail. That, along with lots of other unproductive noise, is what's running through the insecure person's mind. That's why we wrote in our last book, "Insecurity is the most crippling Head-Trash of all. No other leadership obstacle is so deeply rooted."

And few are as disruptive to the friends and family members who have to deal with it.

Case History: Compensation station—Coping mechanisms

Your most recent hire is a terrific salesperson, completely comfortable and confident out in the field, even in what others might consider difficult situations. She asks all the right questions to dig out prospect's motivations and has no fear about following up once, twice, five times to nudge the transaction toward a sale. In fact, she's already closed a few deals in the very short time she's been with the company.

The problems begin when she gets back to the office and has to fit into the company culture. No matter what anyone else says at a meeting, whether or not it pertains to her, she has an opinion, a comment—a long and winding story! The first time you saw this quirk, you thought she was actually attempting to contribute in her own awkward way, and hoped that it was an isolated event. But then it happened again. This time she was making small talk with the president of the company, also known as "The Dark Prince." You overheard her telling him how much she liked his tie. (She actually asked him where he bought it and how much it cost!)

Before this exploded into something worse, you wanted to nip it fast. So you called her into your office and told her, in no uncertain terms, that she needed to think about who she was talking to and whether or not what she was saying was relevant. You were firm, but you weren't shouting. It was a teaching moment, offered as constructive coaching.

The good news? She immediately stopped having inappropriate conversations, as if she had thrown a switch. The bad? She stopped talking altogether for nearly a week, practically going into hiding and not returning calls or emails. She even dodged a few clients and prospects that were calling to give her business. What you interpreted as thoughtless, well-nigh obnoxious overconfidence was actually extreme anxiety and discomfort about fitting in, a coping mechanism. Your attempt at a teaching moment thus hit your very able, but very un-self-confident new hire like a ton of bricks, throwing her off her game.

A scene from the movie "Mean Girls" was playing out daily, with the unpopular girl trying to earn a seat at the lunch table. In short, while it's difficult to talk about insecurity, it's often even more challenging to identify it.

Insecure wherever they are: Eight signs to look for at home and at work

Insecurity is sneaky! It disguises itself in so many different ways, sometimes because the person who has it doesn't know their Achilles' heel. Or because they do know their weakness, and they're running an elaborate scam to fool the rest of the world, including the people closest to them. Here are some of the most common symptoms, and how you're most likely to see them.

1. *"You pissed me off, but I don't know why." Passive-aggressive at home*

   Anger is a difficult emotion under any circumstances. In his groundbreaking book *Wherever You Go, There You Are,* mindfulness therapist Jon Kabat-Zinn writes that anger can deny a person the opportunity to think clearly. "You can feel it cloud the mind. It breeds feelings of aggression and violence—even if the anger is in the service of righting a wrong, or getting something important to happen." So you can imagine that anger and insecurity do not play nicely together. Because the insecure person doesn't have the confidence or the clarity to stand up and say, "I'm angry, *and here's why*," it can produce a "left field" outburst that even surprises the person himself. He can't harness his frustration and express his feelings. Instead, it comes out as an uninformed rage tornado, a force without a source or direction. Or, if the insecure person is gaming you, the explosion's purpose is veiled, because the aggrieved party is actually angry about something other than the topic at hand. Either way, it's passive-aggressive and counterproductive. Be wary of the inexplicably angry friend or family member, and look for deeper meaning.

2. *"Whatever you say, Dear." Never expresses an opinion*
   The other side of the passive-aggressive coin, while easier to recognize, is not much better. Spouses and family who yes you to death, who can't come up with their own point of view when asked their opinion, are substituting submissiveness for involvement. The henpecked husband, the too-willing wife, the overly compliant kid—they all suffer from a lack of self-confidence and don't think they deserve to be taken seriously. And from there, it's not a far jump before they, too, become passive-aggressive. After all, they're also too unsure to say what's really on their minds. When their opinion arrives, often through a side door, the indirect and delayed hostility boils over and looks like something other than what it really is.

3. *"My child will conquer it for me." Passing down the insecurity*
   One of psychoanalyst Carl Jung's primary contributions to psy-
   chology was the concept of projection, the observation that we
   project onto someone else whatever it is that we need or want
   them to be. Nowhere is that more powerful and potentially
   hazardous than when a parent pushes a child into situations
   to compensate for his or her own perceived shortcomings and
   failed dreams. True, if the kid has some talent and a passion for
   the parent's interest, that's being supportive. But we've all seen
   the stage mom who steers her disinterested daughter through
   endless auditions, pageants, and talent competitions. Or the
   hard-driving sports dad who is training a reluctant quarter-
   back instead of raising a self-motivated son. Insecurity then
   becomes a bad inheritance, a hand-me-down in which parents
   unconsciously pass along their own self-doubts in pushing
   their progeny to achieve.

4. *"I told you I was trouble. I know that I'm no good." Self-*
   sabotage at work
   Why do otherwise competent people go out of their way
   to undermine themselves? What compels them to ignore a
   boss's repeated warnings, insult a loved one, or forget the one
   thing they needed to say to win the account? Certain they'll
   be revealed as the inadequate poseurs they think they are,
   people with "impostor syndrome" often "prove" their unworthiness with self-sabotaging conduct. In their 1978 book,
   The Impostor Phenomenon Among High Achieving Women:
   Dynamics and Therapeutic Intervention, clinical psychologists Pauline Clance and Suzanne Imes coined the phrase
   to describe people who believe they are frauds, despite what
   they've achieved. The insecure person is prone to feeling, and

then somehow confirming, a negative self-judgment. As if to say, "See, I really am a failure."

5. *"Don't grow without me": The insecure manager*
Want to know if one of your managers is insecure? Take a look at the person's team. If the staff is underdeveloped, stifled, kept out of the loop, it could be that their boss doesn't have the self-confidence to advocate for their growth. Worse yet, the insecure executive actually desires people to stay right where they are. Business as usual is less threatening than real growth.

6. *"You work for me, so I get the credit!"*
Insecure leaders have a hard time with kudos, unless they can keep them for themselves. Even if they're unentitled, even if sharing would energize their staff, insecure bosses don't give credit where credit is due. This leaves their teams uninspired and resentful, especially when they're asked to step up and do more. "The insecure boss has to constantly be reassured that he or she is okay. It's a well that can never be filled, because it's always leaking," Tim says. "And with the wrong comment, it can be drained just like that."

7. *"You can't handle the truth!" Unable to hear constructive criticism*
All of us need a little coaching from time to time. "Feedback is a gift, especially if it's delivered respectfully and could lead to a better outcome," Tish says. "We should welcome it." The opposite of receptiveness, defensiveness is a common reflex with insecure people. They strike back instead of taking counsel, primed to pounce because the message they always

hear is, "You're not good enough," versus, "Here's how you can grow."

8. *Building your ego while belittling others*
Clients may not always be right, but is it really a good idea to make them feel wrong? The same goes for your staff, your spouse, your children, and other family members. And yet, that's exactly what some insecure people do, employing pre-emptive attacks to diminish anyone who doesn't share their point of view. That kill-or-be-killed mentality, however, also eliminates the opportunity of building trust, the backbone of any successful relationship, whether at home or at the office.

Behind the Scenes with Tish & Tim: Insecurity Anecdote— The insecure parent

Earlier, we mentioned that insecurity can be tricky to identify. Even a trained professional can find it difficult to discern the difference between insecurity and, say, paranoia. What happens, then, when an insecure behavior appears to be an act of parental guidance? To illustrate the point, Tish describes parents who, with the best intentions, have overbooked their children's lives. In pre-school, they have the child attending every possible play date, with a social calendar to rival a politician raising campaign funds. In junior high, they then make sure the child attends all the key social functions, pushing them toward the "popular" kids. All to make sure they're well liked.

The parents may tell themselves they're expressing their love for their children. But they're really expressing their own inse-curity as people in the world. These parents want their children to be successful socially to compensate emotionally and psychologically for their own feelings of being unlikable and unpopular. That's a bad recipe for parent and child alike. "If you have a chronic feeling of insecurity, you can transfer it to your children," Tish said. "Making sure your child hangs out with the right friends, is seen in the right places, gets into the right schools—all the how-it-looks stuff stems from insecurity. What's been labeled 'Helicopter Parenting' is often a form of insecurity."

Prudence versus doubt: What's the difference? It's a list!

It's important to know the difference between insecurity and its noble cousin, prudence. At first glance they may seem identical. For example, delaying an impulsive action in favor of added research can be the best possible decision, a prudent step in the right direction. It can also be a stall tactic. Prudence and insecurity are vastly different. The proof is in the outcome.

An Insecurity Checklist and Comparison

HOW TO IDENTIFY INSECURITY HEADTRASH IN SOMEONE YOU KNOW.

INSECURE PEOPLE . . .	PRUDENT PEOPLE . . .
Tell you immediately why a project can't be done.	Won't make a commitment at the beginning of a decision process.
Without gaining insights, offer answers.	Ask probing questions to get more data before offering a point of view.

(continued)

INSECURE PEOPLE . . .	PRUDENT PEOPLE . . .
When the going gets rough, get up and leave. Stay out of the picture.	Take the lead and stay with a project through completion.
Can't invite anyone to the party.	Encourage involvement by seeking help and input from others.
Grab credit without thinking.	Share credit always.
Are certain no one else is up to the task.	Look for help to share the workload.

HeadTrash Alert! A Quick Quiz on Insecurity

TO ASSESS WHETHER SOMEONE YOU KNOW HAS INSECURITY HEADTRASH, USE THE FOLLOWING QUIZ:

	Never	Sometimes	Often	Always
1. When assigned a new task, the first comment is, "I can't do this."				
2. Has thought or said, "I was assigned this task because my boss is testing me."				
3. Obsesses over deadlines and believes most are too severe to meet.				
4. Hates presenting at executive meetings.				
5. Is reluctant to hire people who have better credentials than they have for fear of training their replacement.				

(continued)

	Never	Sometimes	Often	Always
6. Finds it difficult to receive feedback.				
7. Often puts off projects hoping they will just go away.				

If you checked "often" or "always" three or more times, the person in question probably has insecurity HeadTrash.

I (Tish) see insecurity playing out with couples, where a husband is too uncomfortable to say what's really on his mind to his wife. So they can't make progress on anything meaningful to them.

And I (Tim) think there's the other side, where the wife knows her husband is insecure, so she doesn't speak up because she's afraid of his reaction—his anger, or guilt, or sulking. So she avoids conversations on serious issues.

Penny's Perspective

Insecurity and the desire to avoid confrontation cause meaningful issues to be ignored. This lack of communication has a compounding effect; it leads to false assumptions. Instead of asking questions and having discussions, people assume they know what would be said. But imagining a fight can be much worse than having it, and by the time the inevitable conflict does take place, it is 10 times the size that it needs to be. This can then have a negative impact on relationships.

Will, skill, resilience: How insecure people overachieve and fool the world

It's a mystery, an oxymoron. Consider the following high performing individuals:

- The vice president of a Fortune 500 company

- A successful entrepreneur launching a new product

- The go-to head of the household, running the family

With achievements that would suggest otherwise, how can we classify these people as insecure? Shouldn't insecurity stop them cold in their tracks?

Oddly enough, it could actually be contributing to their current success. What we've seen repeatedly is that many insecure people attempt to compensate for lack of self-worth by out working everyone else. The fear of being revealed as incapable drives them to push harder and bounce back faster. Naturally, that gains recognition from their superiors, who then promote them. They may earn promotions, kudos, and rewards. But what they don't get is relief from their nagging sense of unworthiness. In fact, their sense of unworthiness will likely get even worse as they advance and gain more responsibility, more staff to manage, more critical decisions to make. Pressure to perform at a higher level only increases the volume of the noise in their heads.

AN EXCERPT FROM OUR FIRST HEADTRASH BOOK

Share this section on how to deal with insecurity

Replacing Old Tapes: Overcoming the HeadTrash of Insecurity Moving From Self Doubt to Self Confidence

As remarkable as this may sound, insecure people usually don't see how self-destructive they really are. While most are aware of their insecurities, they view the behavior that accompanies it as justifiable self-defense, workplace jiu-jitsu that keeps them from being "discovered" for the frauds they think they are. They're the first people to undervalue their achievements with phrases like, "Well, I was lucky," or "Yes, but anyone could have done that."

How do you get out of this morass of insecurity? You must take an accurate self-inventory in order to see yourself as you really are. Ask yourself, "What empirical evidence do I have that I am not good enough?" Make a list of your strengths, because you have them. At the same time list your weaknesses, because you have them, too. Seek the feedback of others through a 360-degree evaluation and/ or ask your manager and colleagues for input. Insecure leaders are often so caught up in their own "stuff" that they require input from others to provide a "reality check." Once you get comfortable with who you really are, you'll be able to see how to cultivate your strengths and compensate for your areas of weakness. And then you can build a team that will complement you so that teamwork becomes a way to success, and not the enemy.

The first step to seeing yourself for who you really are is reversing and improving the basic conversations you have with yourself. You must turn self-trashing into self-respecting, based on the facts and not the drama. Say things like:

- "I can do this!"

- "I'm not a victim."

- "Maybe I'm overreacting."

- "I like a good challenge."

Repeat and repeat and repeat to yourself the positive thoughts and feelings you want to experience, based on your actual accomplishments to date. Reach out to a trusted colleague or coach, if you have one, to remind yourself of your recent accomplishments and victories. This should help you to reprogram the way you think about yourself, so that you can begin to believe the positive truth. Of course, this reprogramming has to work against decades of emotional self-denigration.

Advising the person with the HeadTrash of insecurity

Forgive us for stating the obvious: *the person you're about to counsel is insecure.* That means—whether you're dealing with a co-worker, family member or friend—you have to think about the way you deliver your message. There's a method to saying the things that need to be heard by the people who don't want to hear them.

START WITH POSITIVE FEEDBACK

The goal is to be understood, and then for your words to initiate change. So start with a message anyone would want to hear. Offer some positive feedback. Recognize something that this person is doing that's working. Before you identify the hard issues, begin with some good news. Think of it as softening the ground in advance of sowing the seeds.

COME FROM A SENSE OF CURIOSITY VERSUS ENTITLED ANGER

"Doctor, heal thyself." Before you can defuse someone else, you first have to defuse yourself. That means not allowing the other person's "stuff" to trigger yours. Otherwise, you'll get nowhere. The key is to come from a place of curiosity, of actually trying to understand this person and his emotional make up. One of the key tenets of Buddhism is the concept of "non-judgment," approaching every situation, especially challenging ones, with a blank slate. It's not easy, especially when a person has a history with you. However, it's far more productive to initiate a difficult discussion from a place of curiosity, seeking to understand. Ask questions instead of labeling. Then you come across as genuinely trying to help the other person versus attacking them. And you'll have a much better chance getting through.

NURTURINGLY CONFRONT

When you're ready to have a sit-down with an insecure person, tone is everything—and we do mean everything. The level of your voice, the speed of your delivery, the words you choose will all send strong cues to the hypersensitive insecure person on the other side of the message. The slightest hint of anger or resentment will send unwanted signals, and probably generate unwanted reactions. To "nurturingly confront" is to do it with kindness, with the intent to create a space for acceptance. The goal is not to accuse, but to inspire positive growth.

DELIVER THE GIFT IN PERSON

Earlier in this book, Tish said, "Feedback is a gift." And it's always best to deliver a gift in person. That way, you can see the other person's reaction, and then respond accordingly. In the era of digital communications, the temptation is to fire off an email or a text, especially in the heat of the moment, or because you want everything documented. But that's wrong for so many reasons, one of which is tip 5.

MAKE COACHING A TWO-WAY CONVERSATION

When Moses delivered the Ten Commandments, legend has it there was no room for discussion. It was pretty much, "Here's what God said. Next topic." Every other set of personal recommendations, however, works best when there's give and take, when the receiver participates. Yes, you can lead the dialogue, and be the change agent to encourage growth. But be prepared to listen to another view from the person you're talking to, and hear them out fairly. There's always more than one side to an issue, and it's your obligation to hear the other perspectives.

GO DIRECTLY TO THE PERSON WITH YOUR CONCERNS

This is one time where you really need to keep your own counsel. Never address a problem with a family member or teammate before talking to the person you're having issues with. Denigration focus groups, where you query staff or family members about someone's misbehavior, have a way of getting back to that person. The last thing an insecure person should be thinking is that you've been gathering opinions behind their back, and building a case against them.

BE SPECIFIC ABOUT GOALS AND LAY OUT A PLAN TOGETHER

Insecure people have a lot of noise in their heads. So even though you may be speaking calmly about the issues you'd like to address, the insecure recipient on the other end could be wailing and gnashing internally, screaming at himself and not totally processing your thoughts. So, it might be helpful—especially in a work setting—to work out a road map of check-in meetings and milestones. This way, you set the stage for change, and then take it a step at a time.

Overcoming the HeadTrash of insecurity: Changing perspective

In our last book, we said that insecure people are the first ones to undervalue their accomplishments. Pay them a compliment and you'll hear them say, "Well, I caught a break," or "Anyone could have done that." But in their case, it's neither false modesty nor genuine humility. They often believe it was a stroke of luck that led to their success. Even though they may be aware of their insecurity, they justify the behavior that accompanies it as essential to dealing with the challenges they face.

One thing you can do to help is to urge them to take a true self-inventory, *to see themselves as they really are.* Have them make a list of their strengths and weaknesses. And then encourage them to seek the feedback of others. As insecure people grow comfortable with who they really are, they'll become better able to develop their strengths and lessen their weaknesses.

7

Paranoia—Uncertainty Is the Only Certainty

"He's grueling to be with. Draining. No matter what I say or do, he doubts me, and he thinks I have an ulterior motive. He wants to know everywhere I'm going, and expects me to explain why. I don't know how much longer I can live this way."

There is no reassuring the paranoid person, no conversation convincing enough to put his mind totally at ease. If you're living or working with someone who is paranoid, the best you can hope for is a momentary truce, a *temporary* cessation of hostilities until the next round of emotional mortar fire. Which makes one wonder: where does all that energy and anguish come from? What is the source of the negative life force that drives the paranoid person?

Actually, it starts from a level of distrust the rest of us can't possibly fathom. At soul level, imprinted in his molecular structure, the paranoid *knows* that nothing is as it seems, and that the entire world and its inhabitants are against him. The paranoid person has misgivings and suspicions about everything, and everyone. And we do mean everyone—including, unfortunately, the very people he loves. In fact, often the paranoid person distrusts loved ones most of all. There's a certain logic to that. After all, the people who know us best can for that very reason often wound us the most deeply.

"I know you said you'd love and cherish me forever.
But what exactly do you mean by that?"

Case History: Paranoia at home—Life in the hot seat

The district attorney is questioning the suspect again, interrogating you about why you came home a few minutes late. He began the investigation by asking for a list of names of all the people you were with, repeating each one back to you slowly, as if he was taking a mental inventory while evaluating the accuracy of your statement. The inquest moved on to what restaurant you chose and why. After a cursory conversation about what you had to eat and whether you enjoyed it, he revealed his real line of inquiry.

"Don't they have a band there?" he asked. Of course he knew the answer in advance. Yes, they have a band. This is Friday Ladies Night Out, one of the few evenings you get to breathe freely, and hang with your girl gang. It's dinner, drinks, and laughs, letting your hair down with close friends you've known since high school. You've been doing this once a month for the two years that you've been married. Honestly, you now live for these moments of freedom. And sometimes you do pick a place that has live music.

"Did you dance?" Another question whose answer he could anticipate. He knows you like to dance, and that you sometimes go to this particular restaurant to see the band and kick it out with the girls. Just as you were nodding yes, he bored in. *"Who were you dancing with? What were the songs? For how long?"* It felt like you were on the witness stand for an hour.

Then he sprung the real question, exposing the point of the examination:

"Did you dance with any guys?"

"No!" you said. You told him you would never dance with anyone but the girls.

His tone instantly turning conversational. "That's what I figured. I was just curious. I hope you had a good time," he said.

He was smiling, but the tension hung in the air, thick as a fog. He had pushed too far, revealing his lack of trust in you. It would be weeks before the sting of that episode subsided. He had a crossed a line, and you didn't know how to tell him how you felt, for fear of triggering another incident.

Paranoia: Seven signs to look for at home and at work

If you live or work with a paranoid person, you probably need this book every bit as much as the person you'd like to help. The reason is that paranoid people's minds are always working, on red alert for any threats to their security. And should their internal sentry perceive a challenge, the paranoid person begins persuading and manipulating. Before you know it, you, too, are wrapped up in their story and doing their bidding, carrying out a plan just to keep the other person happy. They expend a lot of energy, yours and theirs, getting their way. To get them help, and to get your own life back, you need to know the difference between a real need and a paranoid con.

1. *Trust goes bust and collaboration collapses*
   Families, friendships, and romantic relationships should be trust factories, naturally generating goodwill and common causes. And businesses work better when there's a sense of collective conviction. The paranoid person, conversely, is the stone in the sprocket, the doubter whose built-in suspicion stops him or her from supporting other people, even when they have mutual interests and a mutual goal.

2. *It's my story and you must play a supporting role*
   Paranoid people are narcissistic recruiters. Without thinking twice, they involve everyone around them in their personal

conspiracies, justifying their worldview to anyone who will listen—as if you had a choice. They cajole and orchestrate as much as they can to protect themselves. When you see hours of your life disappearing because you're on the other side of numerous detailed rationalizations and machinations, you're in the presence of paranoia.

"The amount of time you put in is a big tip off," says Tish. "It's so much work. You spend hours of your life in long-winded conversations, proving that you love them, or disproving some crazy theory. It's way more than most people want to manage."

3. *Picking "B" players to make themselves feel better*
Look closely and you'll recognize the paranoid manager. She's the one with the subpar performers, hired to make her feel more comfortable about herself. Or the superstars she keeps in line with KBG-worthy incriminations and inquiries.

At home, he's the family member who makes severe emotional demands of his relatives, cajoling them to prove their love by extracting favors. "Paranoia on the home front comes with more emotional baggage. There are 'shoulds' and 'oughts'," Tim says. "They have expectations that heighten discomfort even more for everyone who has to live with them."

4. *It's showtime all the time*
The insecure person is trying to hide his fears, while the paranoid person needs you to know what he's thinking and feeling 24/7. Paranoid people are assertive. And should one be in a position of influence—say your boss, your business peer or even your sister-in-law—he or she can sow a lot of unrest.

At work, even if this person is not a manager or leader,

it's a costly distraction, with no real payoff for the rest of the group. Questions, probes, and sudden meetings are the norm, draining you day by day.

At home, she's the high maintenance member of the family, stirring up a storyline around an imagined slight or threat. The stakes are high, even when there are no stakes, because paranoia is ever present.

5. *Working hard and producing nothing*
Ever notice people who are very busy politicking, temperature taking, grandstanding, and putting out PR? They seem very involved, very important. But if you take a second look, you can see their whirlwinds don't generate much of anything productive. It's all about self-protection, all the time.

6. *Nothing ventured. Nothing gained—Ever*
In business, the biggest risk is not taking a smart risk to generate growth. The same is true in our personal lives when we avoid relationships, not trusting people long enough to build a healthy and rewarding bond. The paranoid, however, just can't bring herself to try a new project. And new people represent new threats. A little discretion and caution are good practices. But the sure sign of a paranoid is someone who trusts nothing long enough to set the wheels in motion.

7. *Sees personal insults in every comment and email*
If your family member spends a huge portion of her life feeling offended, reading affronts into casual comments, beware. Every glance and conversation becomes a diabolical message to be deciphered and responded to. Watch out when someone habitually says things such as, "What did he mean by that?",

"Did you think it was strange when X did Y?", or "Tell me what this sounds like to you."

In the era of digital communications, the paranoid employee is hard at work misconstruing each text or email to mean something dire, insulting, or threatening. No set of words is as it seems; nothing can be taken at face value because their job is always in jeopardy.

Penny's Perspective

Round and round in circles they go

People suffering from paranoia are tired from the scenarios they run in their heads. It leaves them impaired, and exhausted, which increases the paranoia. A cop who follows a car long enough will eventually find something to be cited. That same premise reinforces the paranoid person's behavior. If she's determined to find a problem, surely she will. In the meantime, she's delaying action and slowing down growth.

The other side of this coin is "the blinder effect." You look but you don't see. The person's paranoia prevents him from observing what's right in front of his eyes, because his "story" obscures reality.

Behind the Scenes with Tish & Tim: Paranoia Anecdote— The paranoid bachelor

Lee was a brilliant contrarian. At the office, he had a knack for seeing things differently from everyone else around him, anticipating senior management pushbacks before they occurred, sensing a competitive threat and having numerous defensive and offensive postures in place ahead of time. Combine that with the chutzpah of someone certain of his point of view, and everyone around him thought he was a formidable presence in the office. Actually, too formidable. The truth was that most of the prognostications and anticipations were about one topic: Lee. His genius and manic drive were spent on protecting his career and defending his position in the company. Hired to work with this person to help him jettison his self-defeating behaviors, Tim labored to understand what was driving Lee's HeadTrash.

"It turns out that his family had survived the Japanese internment camps. Everything made sense the second I heard his story," said Tim. "His father's family was living in California at the time of World War II, and Lee said they were rounded up like criminals. They were forced to leave their homes and jobs, and confined in what were often harsh conditions. As a result Lee's father raised him with the certainty that no one besides family could ever be trusted."

The ripple effect of Lee's upbringing showed up everywhere, Tim now saw. "At work, his direct reports started every briefing with, 'I want to tell you something, but calm down.' He would see people avoiding him in public settings, literally avoiding him, because they knew every conversation was a battle.

"And his personal life was no better. He portrayed himself as something of a playboy, but the truth was that he was terribly lonely and ready to start a family. But he had no clue how to get out of his own way. When we met, Lee said, 'I'm exhausted. I don't want to live this way anymore.'"

We helped Lee to see that he was not his parents and that he lived in a different time and place. We then helped him to begin the process of trusting others enough to allow them to build a relationship with him based on reality and not on Lee's assumptions. Over time he succeeded in these efforts and was able to form lasting relationships in both his personal and professional life.

Paranoia versus insecurity: "I don't trust you" versus "I don't trust me"

To the amateur genealogist, paranoia and insecurity may seem like identical twins. Sure, both are born of the DNA of doubt, but in our experience they're more like second cousins. Although they share a family history, they barely look and act alike out in the world. In fact, they can be polar opposites.

"Insecure people are always trying to please others," says Tish. "They're trying to figure out what someone else is thinking so they can present themselves in the most flattering light." Insecurity, in other words, is reactive. Paranoid people, however, are the opposite. "They're certain they already know what the rest of the world is thinking, which is that they're out to get them. So they're going to push their agenda, because their best defense is a good offense. They're aggressive. They take a narrow view and globalize."

At work, the threat perceived by the paranoid is fairly straightforward, usually amounting to the belief that someone is trying to jeopardize a job or stand in the way of a promotion.

In a family situation, however, it's usually more intimate and subtle. "There could be paranoia that a relative thinks negatively of me, doesn't believe in me, doesn't love me, doesn't understand me, doesn't support me," Tim says of the paranoid person. And then the stakes get ratcheted even higher as family members play the relationship card. That serves up a toxic HeadTrash cocktail: paranoia mixed with a heaping splash of guilt.

Consider, for example, the 70ish mother who berates her middle-aged daughter for accepting a job. What should be a cause for celebration becomes a guilt Ping-Pong tournament, because under it all, mom is paranoid that her adult daughter is abandoning her. Even though her daughter visits daily, mom is certain that her daughter doesn't love her. So she's working at making everyone around her crazy and resentful.

AN EXCERPT FROM OUR FIRST HEADTRASH BOOK

Share this section on how to deal with paranoia

Paranoia: The distorted lens that taints everything

As with every other type of HeadTrash, the paranoid person brings his special set of panic goggles to every situation. He doesn't need a precipitating cause to arouse suspicion because it's there all the time, operating in the background. Did someone ask you to write a report about a project you're wrapping up? Well, clearly that person is out to get you. What are they going to do with the report, and how will it reflect on you? Was a meeting held without you while you were on vacation? That can't be good, because it gave people an opportunity to talk behind your back and advance their plans ahead of yours.

This perennial state of victimhood stands in the way of getting things done, and is usually draining for the paranoid person scrambling to put his finger in every perceived leak. It also saps the people around him, who are running around with the hoses, attempting to extinguish the paranoid's fictional fires. This malady can actually increase as one rises into more senior positions. The more senior the role, the more isolated a leader can feel because being at the helm of a business requires a certain level of separation from "the troops." As the old saying goes, "It's lonely at the top," and it is not uncommon for folks in such a position to become suspicious. A classic example from history of a leader whose suspiciousness got the best of him is President Richard Nixon, whose paranoia led him directly into the Watergate controversy. Nixon got so good at convincing himself of his paranoid thoughts that his behaviors killed his credibility and ultimately brought down his presidency.

Two types of paranoid responses: I do everything; I do nothing

The internal experience of business paranoia, obsessive worry about non-factual events and perceived threats, is similar for most executives who wrestle with it. But its external effects—how it manifests itself in their behavior—can be very different.

For some, paranoia is a rocket launcher that drives them into hyperactive mode to cover their tracks and manage conversations, setting multiple events into motion continually. Tim had a client who was constantly reacting to perceived slights to his department or him personally. He was like the circus performer who is trying to keep all the plates in the air. Even though this person was good at his job, and had a good reputation, he was exhausted all the time.

On the flip side are leaders whose paranoia prevents them from doing anything at all. Their thoughts paralyze them to the point that they cannot make a productive decision. They avoid taking a stand on anything, so as not to give anyone ammunition against them.

A Paranoia Checklist and Comparison

HOW TO IDENTIFY PARANOIA HEADTRASH IN SOMEONE YOU KNOW.

PARANOID PEOPLE . . .	TRUSTING PEOPLE . . .
Are suspicious of everything.	Are cautious when needed.
Can't build trust because they won't share information.	Gain confidence by engaging team and family members.
Micromanage every situation.	Empower people to work autonomously to achieve goals.
Are jealous that successful people make them look bad.	Celebrate success and feel there's enough for everyone.
Stick their noses in everyone else's business for fear of "missing" something.	Focus on specific projects to achieve agreed goals.
Change direction randomly for self-protection.	Follow through on plans and promises.
Are guarded and combative when experiencing a perceived threat.	Are direct, open, and emotionally balanced.

Head Trash Alert! A Quick Quiz on Paranoia

TO ASSESS WHETHER SOMEONE YOU KNOW HAS PARANOIA HEADTRASH, USE THE FOLLOWING QUIZ:

	Never	Sometimes	Often	Always
1. Spends too much time worrying about what others are thinking versus working on the project.				
2. Hangs on to feelings or resentments long after others say they've moved on.				
3. In meetings or family gatherings, is overly concerned about someone's reaction long after the event.				
4. Overreacts when receiving information, fearing that someone is trying to harm them.				
5. Is hesitant to share knowledge and ideas, and distrusts others on the team.				
6. Panics and thinks the worst when someone says, "I've heard a lot about you!"				
7. Finds new reasons to worry about issues that seemed to already have been resolved.				
8. Misinterprets friendly teasing or joking as a threat.				

If you checked "often" or "always" three or more times, the person in question probably has paranoia HeadTrash.

> *I (Tish) now realize that many people we call "High Maintenance" are actually acting out of a level of paranoia. They require so much attention from others because they're constantly thinking, "Are you really looking out for me? Can I trust you? Do you love me? Are you my friend?"*

> *I (Tim) would point out that in that context, most people would think "high maintenance" is tied to insecurity, which it can be, too. But you make a great point. We write off family members or friends as "High Maintenance" without looking deeper. That's a warning. When you have to put in so much time to maintain a relationship, it may indicate paranoia.*

How do paranoid people succeed in a "hostile" world?

Your honor, let the record show: we never said that paranoia automatically makes a person a failure. In many cases, quite the opposite is true. Lots of paranoid people are successful, in great part, *because* they channel their hyper-awareness. Like human weathervanes detecting a storm brewing, they scramble around the office, the family tree, and the social network, to handle threats and spin them. "It works for a while, maybe forever," Tim says. "But it's exhausting. It eats them up inside. And it keeps them from realizing their full potential."

Advising the person with the HeadTrash of paranoia

Coaching a person who is paranoid is a tricky business. As we said earlier in this chapter, many are smart. They're thinkers, plotters, schemers, and strategists. Their gut instincts are highly developed. In fact, don't be surprised if they anticipate your intervention and have five good reasons why you're wrong, why you're the one at fault. So, as with any sensitive message, how you say it is as important as what you say. And if you sense this assignment is beyond your skills, don't hesitate to suggest outside counseling, although you should expect resistance when you do.

ASK GOOD QUESTIONS

To get inside the head of your paranoid friend or family member, and encourage them to hear something other than their own noise, you'll need a solid line of interrogation. The goal is to get them to consider a thought process outside of their reflexive, self-protective box. In short, you'll need to ask probing, disruptive questions:

- Are the things that set you off real or imagined?

- What are you actually upset about?

- Is this a current problem or something from the past?

- What's truly at stake for you?

EMPLOY PATIENCE AND COMPASSION TO GET TO THE ROOT OF THE PROBLEM

Didn't we say that paranoid people could be "high maintenance?" Don't you recall spending hours hearing out and challenging conspiracy theories? Well, you're about to put in more time, but this time with a specific goal. Your objective is to help your team member or loved one get to the core of her issue. You know it won't be easy. In fact, it might be frustrating. And it might require a trained professional to pick up where you leave off. But it is essential if this person is going to grow beyond her own walls.

STEP BACK. DON'T LET THEIR PARANOIA DRAW YOU IN

Few people make their case more effectively than a true-believing paranoid. The proof is in how well they get others to go along with their point of view, which on second and third glance may seem a little wacky. But in order for you to be effective, you'll have to develop some immunity to their powers of persuasion. That gets easier when you realize that everything they say comes from a position of self-persecution.

HAVE SOME GOALS, MILESTONES, AND MEASURES

The beauty of metrics is that they're dispassionate. They don't take sides, don't respond to a brilliant presentation, and don't succumb to charm. The person who's agreed to work on their personal progress is either hitting their goals or not. Which is why getting them to agree on a set of objectives in advance is so important.

FOCUS ON WINNING THE WAR, NOT THE DAILY BATTLES

By the time you've gotten to the stage where you're ready to confront someone's sore spots, there's usually a lot at stake. It could be as serious as a marriage at risk; or perhaps a job is on the line. No doubt you've already experienced dozens of skirmishes. And there will be more. But your goal, as the person bringing issues to head, is to keep your eyes on the prize. Stay above the fray, and work effectively for long-term change.

SUGGESTING THERAPY COULD BE A GIFT

Forgive us for being repetitive on this point, but it's that important, and that difficult to do. No one wants to be the person who says, "You need help." It's uncomfortable, and suggests that someone requires treatment at a more serious level. And by nature of who he is and how he behaves, someone who's paranoid may be extremely difficult to lead to counseling. And yet, an independent clinician or executive coach might be the only person who can get through his defenses. Objectivity and detachment are two key ingredients in dealing with this daunting person effectively.

The most important thing you can do for a paranoid person is to enable them to see that their paranoia is usually the result of seeing everything through their own distorted prism. If you can help that person stand outside their thinking, even for a moment, to see the world the rest of us live in, you'll have done him or her a world of good.

Cleaning Up Your HeadTrash or Helping Others with Theirs Is an Act of Courage

In case you haven't gotten the message by now, let's be clear: everyone has his or her own form of HeadTrash. That includes us, Tish and Tim; that includes you; and that includes anyone you're trying to help see and work through his or her own Head-Trash. But there is a spectrum for HeadTrash from trivial human foible to tragic human flaw. The question is, are these natural tendencies to think and feel in certain ways so counterproductive that they derail people from being their best selves?

Some people are control freaks, so caught up in wanting to manage every detail that they can't let their family members simply live their lives. Others are so insecure or paranoid that they can't get out of their own way to start or finish projects that are worthwhile and important to them. And some people have HeadTrash cocktails, combinations of toxins that keep them from reaching their potential. Consciously or not, people learn these coping mechanisms and lean on the adaptive patterns that they believe are serving them well. Like old friends, these Head-Trashes have been their M.O. for so many years. There's nothing unusual about that. It's human.

So, dear human, this book is for you, for the person who has raised her hand and said, "I know I can be better, and I'm ready to get started." This book is also for anyone who is trying to help someone else get out of their own way, who has people they care about and for whom they want the best. It could be a family member, a friend, or a colleague whose "stuff" is holding him back or driving everyone around him crazy with behaviors he may not even notice.

In all cases, knowledge is power. That expression is not only true in professional situations like job interviews or negotiations, but also when we're on a path of self-realization and improvement. Once you've identified a HeadTrash and recognized how it distorts perceptions and reactions, it's hard to go backwards. You or the person you're working with can no longer pretend it doesn't exist. That awareness can become a call to action, a rallying cry, and a visible starting gate for the journey you or someone you care for is about to take.

So how do we do this, how do we initiate and continue the difficult conversations that pave the path of change? Here are four steps that we've found to be helpful in just about any interaction, whether you're guiding a child to own an unseen tendency, or attempting to manage up and show your boss that there might be better ways of working with you.

1. *Seek first to understand*

   It's best to begin by following the time-proven counsel, "Seek to understand before attempting to be understood." Instead of approaching a challenging conversation with a set of rigid beliefs and packaged prescriptions that you'll deliver in attack mode, arrive inquisitive, eager to learn more, knowing what you know about that person and their behaviors, but with as little judgment as you can muster. In the previous chapter we discussed the Buddhist practice of non-judgment. In the opening of any coaching conversation, trying to understand, keeping that "don't know yet" mind, is always better than laying down the law. Begin a conversation that should lead to mutual agreement versus unleashing a diatribe to be followed rigidly.

2. *Don't text, email, digitally chat, or phone it in*
   In this "I-have-no-time, I-must-record-every-word, I-can-multi-task-this" world, we're always looking for the "optimal" way to do things. Surely you can send a perfectly scripted recommendation online, while having a conference call and checking Facebook, right?

   No, you cannot. Your physical presence, in this era of digital communications, says that something important is about to occur, something that merits a meeting. Anything personal, and potentially uncomfortable, is best done human to human. Despite the changes in social mores and communication technology, you have an obligation to the other person, and yourself, to do this right. And that means having a conversation, in person, where you can have an ongoing interaction.

3. *Say it to face to face, and only face to face*
   What's one of the big benefits of social media? That you can broadcast any message to as many people as you like with the click of a track pad. What's the primary ill of social media? That you can broadcast any message to as many people as you like with the click of a track pad. You may win gossip points by asking extended family, "Are you as annoyed by cousin Mary's controlling tone as I am?" But when it comes time to confront Mary, she'll likely know what's on your mind, and will think

you a jerk for going public. Instead, keep your thoughts to yourself, or restrict them to one trusted outside party who has no personal interaction with the people involved, or incentive to share your private information. News travels, and bad news travels fastest.

4. *Design a success roadmap*
   What does success look like for the person you're working with? Will a brother be less controlling when running the family affairs? Will a wife and parent stop using guilt to push everyone's buttons around her? Get the person you're working with to join you in describing what success will look like, and then together lay out a plan for checking in periodically on progress. This may be tough in day-to-day family environments, but an open acknowledgment that everyone is moving forward with a common goal and blueprint is the best way to keep everyone on track.

Is the pain worth the gain? You bet!

What we can tell you from personal experience is that it's worth the effort. A more authentic, engaged and productive person is already in the wings, waiting for his or her new scripts. We've seen it in our own lives, and we've witnessed it repeatedly with our clients. The path to change always begins with awareness. That often leads to uncomfortable honesty about what needs attention. But from that point on, when people are willing to work on spotting and changing their thoughts and behaviors, they can lessen the grip that anger, arrogance, control, fear, guilt, insecurity, and paranoia have on them. They'll replace those automatic HeadTrash reflexes with new actions that lead to positive results.

And an additional note to anyone reading this who is supporting someone else in their development: we applaud you! You're doing noble work, but you're also doing challenging work. Any change is hard, especially when coaching people with entrenched behaviors. As result, we *highly recommend* you turn to these pages often, and share them with the people you want to help. We also suggest, again, that you look to outside support if needed, be it consulting a therapist, executive coach, social worker, or your spiritual advisor. You may be the person leading the effort, but you don't have to do it alone.

Finally, to learn which HeadTrashes (yes, plural) you or a loved one may need to work on, take our five-minute HeadTrash inventory at http://headtrash911.com/the-headtrash-index/. It's free, it's actually fun and it's highly insightful. You or the person you're helping might be surprised to learn, in detail, what your HeadTrashes really are and where to begin the work.

Also, we offer further perspective on HeadTrash and related matters on our web site and blog (www.HeadTrash911.com), and in our seminar, "HeadTrash: Sweep It, Bag It, Crush It!" To close, we'd like to give you a capsule description of the seminar that also serves as a summary of this book.

HeadTrash: Sweep It, Bag It, Crush It!

SWEEP IT

—The first step on the path to being more effective is to identify your personal HeadTrash and sweep it into the center of your consciousness. This awareness alone will help you begin to manage unwanted behaviors. But sweeping up HeadTrash is demanding work. It requires an open mind and a strong character to recognize your own HeadTrash: emotional honesty about who you are, and the fortitude to be willing to change.

BAG IT

—Once you've identified and accepted your HeadTrash, it's time to eliminate it and put it where it belongs. But before you bag HeadTrash like lawn clippings or fall leaves you need to have a greater understanding of how it exhibits itself and the negative impact it can have on you and your effectiveness as a leader. Bagging it signifies that you have been able to contain and isolate the counterproductive emotional and mental patterns that generate HeadTrash. Bagging it means learning to recognize situations where your HeadTrash may come into play, defusing the situation before it becomes problematical, and replacing HeadTrash behavior with more appropriate, productive behavior.

CRUSH IT

—Crushing old behaviors takes discipline, desire, and determination. But once you finally rid yourself of success-limiting emotional and mental patterns, you will, for the first time, be able to maximize your skills and utilize your talents to their fullest potential. And then you can truly crush it!

We hope you'll join us in an ongoing conversation about the challenges and rewards of resolving HeadTrash problems. In meantime, we urge you to *sweep it, bag it, crush it!*

ABOUT THE AUTHOR: TISH SQUILLARO

With a goal-oriented and self-confident mindset, Tish creates change. With an instinctual feeling for niche markets and a talent for helping business leaders become "unstuck" and teaching them to make effective decisions, she drives success by focusing her time and commitment to CANDOR Consulting, advising executives with her bold style of training and guidance. She warns clients early: "If you don't feel differently about how you are making decisions after 30 days, I'm doing something wrong."

Tish helps clients leverage human capital to *drive* the success of their businesses rather than simply support it. Drawing on a wealth of knowledge from a broad range of disciplines, she has particular expertise in change management processes, business strategy development, and behavioral and organizational dynamics. Combining sharp problem-solving skills with effective mediation abilities, Tish works primarily with CEOs, executive managers, and boards of directors within organizations at various stages of development, ranging from start-ups to Fortune 500 companies.

The idea for *HeadTrash* was born while Tish was advising a client who was immobilized by fear, guilt, and insecurity. Seeing the fear of failure in her client's eyes was Tish's first personal "HeadTrash" experience. As she was developing her business, Tish often needed other people's confirmation to bolster her self-confidence and rise above insecurity. Learning to manage this type of HeadTrash, which she defines as "patterns of self-defeating feelings and thoughts that can immobilize and keep you stuck," has made her a sought-after advisor to executives and CEOs of companies like GSI Commerce/Ebay, ESAB, and *USA Today*.

Tish is the CEO and Managing Partner of CANDOR Consulting. She is a graduate of the University of Pennsylvania and is a member of the Board of Directors of the Philadelphia-based nonprofit organization ACHIEVEability. Tish lives with her husband and two children in Valley Forge, PA.

ABOUT THE AUTHOR: TIM THOMAS

Timothy I. Thomas began his work in leadership consulting in 2003 as a natural outgrowth of his educational background and his lifelong commitment to helping others succeed.

Tim is a 1987 magna cum laude graduate from the University of Akron and holds two masters degrees, a M.Div. from Princeton Theological Seminary (1990), and a M.S. in Training and Organization Development from Saint Joseph's University in Philadelphia (2002).

As the founding partner of Makarios Consulting (www. makariosconsulting.com), Tim has helped to transform organizations working as a leadership trainer, executive coach, and change management expert. Tim has extensive expertise in training design and delivery, executive coaching, performance consulting, team development, and 360-degree appraisal processes. He also brings to his clients a complete understanding of corporate culture and business processes as well as keen financial acumen, having himself been a vice president at two international banking institutions.

Known for his highly energetic and engaging facilitation style and his strong commitment to helping his clients realize their full potential, Tim has trained or coached thousands of leaders in the art of influencing others to achieve extraordinary results in business and in life.

Tim is the author of two books, *HeadTrash: Cleaning out the Junk that Stands Between You and Success* (2013) and *Leading on Purpose: Sage Advice and Practical Tools for Becoming the Complete Leader* (2014).